A Textbook of Belief Dynamics

A Textbook of Belief Dynamics

Solutions to exercises

by

SVEN OVE HANSSON

Department of Philosophy,
Uppsala University

KLUWER ACADEMIC PUBLISHERS

DORDRECHT / BOSTON / LONDON

A C.I.P. Catalogue record for this book is available from the Library of Congress.

ISBN 0-7923-5328-5 (Solutions PB)

Published by Kluwer Academic Publishers,
P.O. Box 17, 3300 AA Dordrecht, The Netherlands.

Sold and distributed in North, Central and South America
by Kluwer Academic Publishers,
101 Philip Drive, Norwell, MA 02061, U.S.A.

In all other countries, sold and distributed
by Kluwer Academic Publishers,
P.O. Box 322, 3300 AH Dordrecht, The Netherlands.

Printed on acid-free paper

Printed in the Netherlands.

CONTENTS

SOLUTIONS FOR CHAPTER 1 + ...1
SOLUTIONS FOR CHAPTER 2 + ...15
SOLUTIONS FOR CHAPTER 3 + ...43
SOLUTIONS FOR CHAPTER 4 + ...57
SOLUTIONS FOR CHAPTER 5 + ...65

SOLUTIONS FOR CHAPTER 1^+

1. No. For a counterexample, let α and β be logically independent sentences, and let $A = \{\alpha \vee \beta\}$.

2. We need to show that for all β, $\beta \in \mathrm{Cn}(\{\alpha\vee\neg\alpha\})$ holds if and only if $\beta \in \mathrm{Cn}(\varnothing)$.

By deduction, $\beta \in \mathrm{Cn}(\{\alpha\vee\neg\alpha\})$ holds if and only if $\alpha\vee\neg\alpha \rightarrow \beta \in \mathrm{Cn}(\varnothing)$, (since $\alpha\vee\neg\alpha \rightarrow \beta$ is equivalent with β) if and only if $\beta \in \mathrm{Cn}(\varnothing)$.

3. Since $\alpha\rightarrow\beta$ is equivalent with $\neg\alpha\vee\beta$, we have $\mathrm{Cn}(\{\alpha\rightarrow\beta\}) = \mathrm{Cn}(\{\neg\alpha\vee\beta\})$. It therefore follows from Observation 1.17 that $\mathrm{Cn}(\{\neg\alpha \vee \beta\}) = \mathrm{Cn}(\{\neg\alpha\}) \cap \mathrm{Cn}(\{\beta\})$.

4. $\mathrm{Cn}(\{\alpha\rightarrow\beta\}) \cap \mathrm{Cn}(\{\beta\rightarrow\alpha\}) =$
$= \mathrm{Cn}(\{\neg\alpha\vee\beta\}) \cap \mathrm{Cn}(\{\neg\beta\vee\alpha\})$
$= \mathrm{Cn}(\{\neg\alpha\}) \cap \mathrm{Cn}(\{\beta\}) \cap \mathrm{Cn}(\{\neg\beta\}) \cap \mathrm{Cn}(\{\alpha\})$
$= \mathrm{Cn}(\{\alpha\}) \cap \mathrm{Cn}(\{\neg\alpha\}) \cap \mathrm{Cn}(\{\beta\}) \cap \mathrm{Cn}(\{\neg\beta\})$
$= \mathrm{Cn}(\{\alpha\vee\neg\alpha\}) \cap \mathrm{Cn}(\{\beta\vee\neg\beta\})$ (Observation 1.17)
$= \mathrm{Cn}(\varnothing) \cap \mathrm{Cn}(\varnothing)$ (Exercise 2)
$= \mathrm{Cn}(\varnothing)$

5. Suppose that $A \subseteq D \subseteq B \subseteq \mathrm{Cn}(A)$. It follows by monotony from $D \subseteq B$ that $\mathrm{Cn}(D) \subseteq \mathrm{Cn}(B)$.

It also follows by monotony from $B \subseteq \mathrm{Cn}(A)$ that $\mathrm{Cn}(B) \subseteq \mathrm{Cn}(\mathrm{Cn}(A))$. By iteration, $\mathrm{Cn}(\mathrm{Cn}(A)) = \mathrm{Cn}(A)$, so that $\mathrm{Cn}(B) \subseteq \mathrm{Cn}(A)$. It follows by monotony from $A \subseteq D$ that $\mathrm{Cn}(A) \subseteq \mathrm{Cn}(D)$. From $\mathrm{Cn}(B) \subseteq \mathrm{Cn}(A)$ and $\mathrm{Cn}(A) \subseteq \mathrm{Cn}(D)$ we obtain $\mathrm{Cn}(B) \subseteq \mathrm{Cn}(D)$.

From $\mathrm{Cn}(D) \subseteq \mathrm{Cn}(B)$ and $\mathrm{Cn}(B) \subseteq \mathrm{Cn}(D)$ we may conclude that $\mathrm{Cn}(D) = \mathrm{Cn}(B)$.

6. Suppose that $A \subseteq \mathrm{Cn}(B)$. It follows from inclusion that $B \subseteq \mathrm{Cn}(B)$, so that $A \cup B \subseteq \mathrm{Cn}(B)$. By monotony, $\mathrm{Cn}(A \cup B) \subseteq \mathrm{Cn}(\mathrm{Cn}(B))$. By iteration, $\mathrm{Cn}(\mathrm{Cn}(B)) = \mathrm{Cn}(B)$, so that $\mathrm{Cn}(A \cup B) \subseteq \mathrm{Cn}(B)$.

7. For one direction, let $\mathrm{Cn}(B) = \mathrm{Cn}(D)$. We then have $B \subseteq \mathrm{Cn}(B) = \mathrm{Cn}(D)$ and $D \subseteq \mathrm{Cn}(D) = \mathrm{Cn}(B)$.

For the other direction, let $B \subseteq \mathrm{Cn}(D)$ and $D \subseteq \mathrm{Cn}(B)$. It follows by monotony that $\mathrm{Cn}(B) \subseteq \mathrm{Cn}(\mathrm{Cn}(D))$ and by iteration that $\mathrm{Cn}(\mathrm{Cn}(D)) = \mathrm{Cn}(D)$, so that $\mathrm{Cn}(B) \subseteq \mathrm{Cn}(D)$ can be concluded. In the same way it follows by monotony that $\text{Cn}(D) \subseteq \text{Cn}(\text{Cn}(B))$ and by iteration that $\text{Cn}(\text{Cn}(B)) = \text{Cn}(B)$, so that $\text{Cn}(D) \subseteq \text{Cn}(B)$ can be concluded.

8. We need to show that (I) if Cn is a consequence operator, then the formula given in the exercise is satisfied, and (II) if the formula is satisfied, then Cn is a consequence operator.

Part I: It follows from inclusion and iteration that $X \subseteq \text{Cn}(\text{Cn}(X))$. Furthermore, it follows from iteration that $\text{Cn}(\text{Cn}(X)) \subseteq \text{Cn}(X)$ and from monotony that $\text{Cn}(X) \subseteq \text{Cn}(X \cup Y)$.

Part II: We now assume that the formula given in the exercise is satisfied. In order to show that Cn is a consequence operator, we must prove that it satisfies inclusion, monotony, and iteration.

Inclusion follows directly from $X \subseteq \text{Cn}(\text{Cn}(X)) \subseteq \text{Cn}(X)$.

For monotony, suppose that $X \subseteq Y$. Then $Y = X \cup Y$, so that $\text{Cn}(X) \subseteq \text{Cn}(Y)$ follows direclty from $\text{Cn}(X) \subseteq \text{Cn}(X \cup Y)$.

One direction of iteration, namely $\text{Cn}(\text{Cn}(X)) \subseteq \text{Cn}(X)$, is directly given. The other direction follows from inclusion, that has already been obtained.

9. One direction of the desired equivalence is trivial, namely that if Cn = Cn', then $\text{Cn}(\varnothing) = \text{Cn}'(\varnothing)$. For the other direction, suppose that $\text{Cn}(\varnothing) = \text{Cn}'(\varnothing)$. In order to show that Cn = Cn' we need to prove that for all B and α, $\alpha \in \text{Cn}(B)$ if and only if $\alpha \in \text{Cn}'(B)$. Due to symmetry, it is sufficient to show that for all B and α, if $\alpha \in \text{Cn}(B)$, then $\alpha \in \text{Cn}'(B)$.

It follows by compactness from $\alpha \in \text{Cn}(B)$ that there is a finite subset B'' of B such that $\alpha \in \text{Cn}(B'')$. By repeated use of Observation 1.18, $\text{Cn}(B'') = \text{Cn}(\{\&B''\})$. We therefore have $\alpha \in \text{Cn}(\{\&B''\})$. By deduction, $\&B'' \rightarrow \alpha \in \text{Cn}(\varnothing)$. Since $\text{Cn}'(\varnothing) = \text{Cn}(\varnothing)$, we have $\&B'' \rightarrow \alpha \in \text{Cn}'(\varnothing)$.

Now we can perform the same procedure backwards, but on Cn' instead of Cn: It follows by deduction that $\alpha \in \text{Cn}'(\{\&B''\})$. By repeated use of Observation 1.18, we obtain $\text{Cn}'(B'') = \text{Cn}'(\{\&B''\})$, so that $\alpha \in \text{Cn}'(B'')$. By $B'' \subseteq B$ and monotony, $\text{Cn}'(B'') \subseteq \text{Cn}'(B)$, so that $\alpha \in \text{Cn}'(B)$, as desired.

10. Suppose that $\text{Cn}_0(X) \subseteq \text{Cn}_0(Y)$.

It follows from inclusion for Cn_0 that $X \subseteq \text{Cn}_0(X)$. By monotony for Cn, $\text{Cn}(X) \subseteq \text{Cn}(\text{Cn}_0(X))$.

It follows by monotony for Cn that $\text{Cn}(\text{Cn}_0(X)) \subseteq \text{Cn}(\text{Cn}_0(Y))$.

It follows by the supraclassicality of Cn that $\text{Cn}_0(Y) \subseteq \text{Cn}(Y)$. By monotony for Cn, $\text{Cn}(\text{Cn}_0(Y)) \subseteq \text{Cn}(\text{Cn}(Y))$ and by iteration $\text{Cn}(\text{Cn}(Y)) = \text{Cn}(Y)$. so that $\text{Cn}(\text{Cn}_0(Y)) \subseteq \text{Cn}(Y)$.

We now have $\text{Cn}(X) \subseteq \text{Cn}(\text{Cn}_0(X))$, $\text{Cn}(\text{Cn}_0(X)) \subseteq \text{Cn}(\text{Cn}_0(Y))$. $\text{Cn}(\text{Cn}_0(Y)) \subseteq \text{Cn}(\text{Cn}(Y))$, and $\text{Cn}(\text{Cn}(Y)) \subseteq \text{Cn}(Y)$. They combine to $\text{Cn}(X) \subseteq \text{Cn}(Y)$, as desired.

11. In order to prove that Cn_T is a consequence operator, we need to show that it satisfies inclusion, monotony, and iteration.

Inclusion: By the inclusion and monotony properties of Cn_0, $A \subseteq Cn_0(A)$ and $Cn_0(A) \subseteq Cn_0(T \cup A) = Cn_T(A)$.

Monotony: Suppose that $A \subseteq B$. Then $T \cup A \subseteq T \cup B$ and, by the monotony of Cn_0, $Cn_0(T \cup A) \subseteq Cn_0(T \cup B)$, i.e., $Cn_T(A) \subseteq Cn_T(B)$.

Iteration: One direction of iteration follows directly from inclusion. For the other direction of this property, suppose that $\chi \in Cn_T(Cn_T(A))$. Then $\chi \in Cn_0(T \cup Cn_0(T \cup A))$. By inclusion and monotony for Cn_0, $T \subseteq Cn_0(T \cup A)$, so that $T \cup Cn_0(T \cup A) = Cn_0(T \cup A)$. We thus have $\chi \in Cn_0(Cn_0(T \cup A))$ and, by the iteration property for Cn_0, $\chi \in Cn_0(T \cup A)$, i.e. $\chi \in Cn_T(A)$.

Supraclassicality: Let $\chi \in Cn_0(A)$. Then by monotony for Cn_0, $\chi \in Cn_0(T \cup A)$, i.e., $\chi \in Cn_T(A)$.

Deduction: $\psi \in Cn_T(A \cup \{\chi\})$ holds if and only if $\psi \in Cn_0(T \cup A \cup \{\chi\})$, thus (by deduction for Cn_0) if and only if $(\chi \rightarrow \psi) \in Cn_0(T \cup A)$, if and only if $(\chi \rightarrow \psi) \in Cn_T(A)$.

Compactness: Suppose that $\chi \in Cn_T(A)$, i.e., $\chi \in Cn_0(T \cup A)$. By the compactness of Cn_0, there are finite subsets S of T and A' of A such that $\chi \in Cn_0(S \cup A')$. By monotony for Cn_0, $\chi \in Cn_0(T \cup A')$, i.e. $\chi \in Cn_T(A')$.

12. We need to show that Cn' satisfies inclusion, monotony, and iteration.

Inclusion: Let $\alpha \in A$. Then $\alpha \in Cn'(A)$ follows from $\alpha \in Cn(\{\alpha\})$.

Monotony: Suppose that $A \subseteq B$ and $\alpha \in Cn'(A)$. Then there is some $\delta \in A$ such that $\alpha \in Cn(\{\delta\})$. It follows from $A \subseteq B$ that $\delta \in B$, from which we may conclude that $\alpha \in Cn'(B)$.

Iteration: One direction follows directly from inclusion. For the other direction, let $\alpha \in Cn'(Cn'(A))$. Then there is some β such that $\alpha \in Cn(\{\beta\})$ and $\beta \in Cn'(A)$. It follows from $\beta \in Cn'(A)$ that there is some δ such that $\beta \in Cn(\{\delta\})$ and $\delta \in A$.

From $\{\beta\} \subseteq Cn(\{\delta\})$ follows by monotony $Cn(\{\beta\}) \subseteq Cn(Cn(\{\delta\}))$ and by iteration $Cn(\{\beta\}) \subseteq Cn(\{\delta\})$. From this and $\alpha \in Cn(\{\beta\})$ follows $\alpha \in Cn(\{\delta\})$. Since $\delta \in A$. this is sufficient to prove that $\alpha \in Cn'(A)$.

13. $\alpha \vdash \beta$ if and only if $\beta \in Cn(\{\alpha\})$, by deduction if and only if $\alpha \rightarrow \beta \in Cn(\varnothing)$, if and only if $\vdash \alpha \rightarrow \beta$.

14. $\alpha \vdash \beta$ and $\beta \vdash \delta$
$\beta \in Cn(\{\alpha\})$ and $\delta \in Cn(\{\beta\})$
$\{\beta\} \subseteq Cn(\{\alpha\})$ and $\delta \in Cn(\{\beta\})$
$Cn(\{\beta\}) \subseteq Cn(Cn(\{\alpha\}))$ and $\delta \in Cn(\{\beta\})$ (monotony)
$Cn(\{\beta\}) \subseteq Cn(\{\alpha\})$ and $\delta \in Cn(\{\beta\})$ (monotony)

$\delta \in \mathrm{Cn}(\{\alpha\})$
$\alpha \vdash \delta$

15. Suppose that $\alpha \vdash \beta$ and $\beta \vdash \alpha$, i.e., $\beta \in \mathrm{Cn}(\{\alpha\})$ and $\alpha \in \mathrm{Cn}(\{\beta\})$. It follows from $\beta \in \mathrm{Cn}(\{\alpha\})$ that $\{\beta\} \subseteq \mathrm{Cn}(\{\alpha\})$, so that by monotony $\mathrm{Cn}(\{\beta\}) \subseteq \mathrm{Cn}(\mathrm{Cn}(\{\alpha\}))$. By iteration, $\mathrm{Cn}(\mathrm{Cn}(\{\alpha\})) = \mathrm{Cn}(\{\alpha\})$, so that $\mathrm{Cn}(\{\beta\}) \subseteq \mathrm{Cn}(\{\alpha\})$.

In the same way we can also prove that $\mathrm{Cn}(\{\alpha\}) \subseteq \mathrm{Cn}(\{\beta\})$. We may therefore conclude that $\mathrm{Cn}(\{\alpha\}) = \mathrm{Cn}(\{\beta\})$. Thus, for all δ, $\delta \in \mathrm{Cn}(\{\alpha\})$ if and only if $\delta \in \mathrm{Cn}(\{\beta\})$, that is $\alpha \vdash \delta$ if and only if $\beta \vdash \delta$.

16. Suppose that $X \vdash \alpha$ and $X \cup \{\alpha\} \vdash \beta$, i.e., that $\alpha \in \mathrm{Cn}(X)$ and $\beta \in \mathrm{Cn}(X \cup \{\alpha\})$. It follows by deduction from $\beta \in \mathrm{Cn}(X \cup \{\alpha\})$ that $\alpha \rightarrow \beta \in \mathrm{Cn}(X)$. Since α and $\alpha \rightarrow \beta$ truth-functionally imply β, it follows by supraclassicality that $\beta \in \mathrm{Cn}(X)$, that is $X \vdash \beta$.

17. a. Suppose to the contrary that $A \vdash \alpha$. Then $X \cup \{\beta \rightarrow \alpha\} \vdash \alpha$, i.e., by the deduction property $X \vdash (\beta \rightarrow \alpha) \rightarrow \alpha$, or equivalently $X \vdash \alpha \vee \beta$, contrary to the conditions.
b. Directly from $\{\alpha \vee \beta, \beta \rightarrow \alpha\} \vdash \alpha$

18. a. $\{p \vee q, \top\}$ **b.** $\{p \rightarrow q, \top\}$ **c.** $\{p, p \vee q, q \rightarrow p, \top\}$ **d.** $\{\top\}$

19. One direction is trivial: if A is logically closed, then there is some B, namely $B = A$ such that $A = \mathrm{Cn}(B)$.

For the other direction, let B be such that $A = \mathrm{Cn}(B)$. By iteration, $\mathrm{Cn}(\mathrm{Cn}(B)) = \mathrm{Cn}(B)$. By substituting A for $\mathrm{Cn}(B)$ we obtain $\mathrm{Cn}(A) = A$, so that A is logically closed.

20. *Part I*: For one direction of the desired equivalence, we are going to show that if $A \cup B$ is logically closed, then either $A \subseteq B$ or $B \subseteq A$. We are going to prove this implication in its converse form. Thus, we are going to show that if it is not the case that $A \subseteq B$ or $B \subseteq A$, then $A \cup B$ is not logically closed. For this purpose, suppose that that $A \not\subseteq B$ and $B \not\subseteq A$. Our task is to prove that $A \cup B \neq \mathrm{Cn}(A \cup B)$.

It follows from $A \not\subseteq B$ that there is some α such that $\alpha \in A$ and $\alpha \notin B$. Similarly, it follows from that $B \not\subseteq A$ that there is some β such that $\beta \in B$ and $\beta \notin A$. We are going to show (1) that $\alpha \leftrightarrow \beta \in \mathrm{Cn}(A \cup B)$, and (2) that $\alpha \leftrightarrow \beta \notin A \cup B$.

For (1): Since $\alpha \in A$, $\alpha \in A \cup B$. Similarly, since $\beta \in B$, $\beta \in A \cup B$. By truth-functional logic, $\alpha \leftrightarrow \beta \in \mathrm{Cn}(\{\alpha,\beta\})$. Since $\{\alpha,\beta\} \subseteq A \cup B$, monotony for

Cn yields $\text{Cn}(\{\alpha,\beta\}) \subseteq \text{Cn}(A \cup B)$. We therefore have $\alpha \leftrightarrow \beta \in \text{Cn}(A \cup B)$, as desired.

For (2): In order to show that $\alpha \leftrightarrow \beta \notin A \cup B$ it is sufficient to show that $\alpha \leftrightarrow \beta \notin A$ and $\alpha \leftrightarrow \beta \notin B$. In order to show that $\alpha \leftrightarrow \beta \notin A$, suppose to the contrary that $\alpha \leftrightarrow \beta \in A$. Since $\alpha \in A$, and β follows by truth-functional logic from α and $\alpha \leftrightarrow \beta$, it would follow that $\beta \in \text{Cn}(A)$, and – since A is closed under logical consequence – that $\beta \in A$, contrary to the conditions. We may conclude from this contradiction that $\alpha \leftrightarrow \beta \notin A$.

The proof that $\alpha \leftrightarrow \beta \notin B$ is similar. We now know that $\alpha \leftrightarrow \beta \notin A \cup B$.

In summary, we have found a sentence $(\alpha \leftrightarrow \beta)$ that is an element of $\text{Cn}(A \cup B)$ but not an element of $A \cup B$. This is sufficient to prove that $\text{Cn}(A \cup B) \neq A \cup B$, i.e., that $A \cup B$ is not logically closed.

Part II: For the other direction of the desired equivalence, suppose that either $A \subseteq B$ or $B \subseteq A$. If $A \subseteq B$, then $A \cup B = B$, and the logical closure of $A \cup B$ follows from that of B. Similarly if $B \subseteq A$, then $A \cup B = A$, and the logical closure of $A \cup B$ follows from that of A.

21. Only c, d and e are $\{p, p \vee q\}$-closed. In a and b, $p \vee q$ is missing.

22. For one direction, let $B_1 \subset B_2$. Then $\text{Cn}(B_1) \subseteq \text{Cn}(B_2)$ follows directly from $B_1 \subseteq B_2$. Suppose that $\text{Cn}(B_1) = \text{Cn}(B_2)$. Since B_1 and B_2 are A-closed, we then have $B_1 = A \cap \text{Cn}(B_1) = A \cap \text{Cn}(B_2) = B_2$, contrary to $B_1 \subset B_2$. It follows from this contradiction that $\text{Cn}(B_1) \neq \text{Cn}(B_2)$, and since we have already proved that $\text{Cn}(B_1) \subseteq \text{Cn}(B_2)$ we can conclude that $\text{Cn}(B_1) \subset \text{Cn}(B_2)$.

The other direction follows from Observation 1.30.

23. Let $c(B_1) = c(B_2)$. We then have $\text{Cn}(B_1) = \text{Cn}(c(B_1)) = \text{Cn}(c(B_2)) = \text{Cn}(B_2)$. Since B_1 and B_2 are A-closed subsets of A, we can therefore derive: $B_1 = A \cap \text{Cn}(B_1) = A \cap \text{Cn}(B_2) = B_2$.

24. Let A_1 and A_2 be B-closed subsets of B. We are going to show that A_1 is A_2-closed, i.e., that $\text{Cn}(A_1) \cap A_2 \subseteq A_1$.

Since $A_2 \subseteq B$, we have $\text{Cn}(A_1) \cap A_2 \subseteq \text{Cn}(A_1) \cap B$. Since A_1 is B-closed, we also have $\text{Cn}(A_1) \cap B \subseteq A_1$. It follows that $\text{Cn}(A_1) \cap A_2 \subseteq A_1$, i.e., that A_1 is A_2-closed. In the same way we can prove that A_2 is A_1-closed. It follows that A_1 and A_2 are mutually closed.

25. Suppose that A and B are closed under implication. We need to show that $A \cap B$ is also closed under implication.

Let α and β be elements of $A \cap B$. Then $\alpha \in A$ and $\beta \in A$, and by the closure under implication of A, $\alpha \rightarrow \beta \in A$. In the same way it follows that

$\alpha\rightarrow\beta \in B$. From $\alpha\rightarrow\beta \in A$ and $\alpha\rightarrow\beta \in B$ we may conclude that $\alpha\rightarrow\beta \in A\cap B$.

26. a. $\{p,q\}\perp p\&q = \{\{p\},\{q\}\}$
b. $\{p,q,r\}\perp p\&q = \{\{p,r\},\{q,r\}\}$
c. $\{q\}\perp p\&q = \{\{q\}\}$
d. $\{p, q\vee r, q\vee\neg r\}\perp p\&q = \{\{p, q\vee r\},\{p, q\vee\neg r\},\{q\vee r, q\vee\neg r\}\}$
e. $\{p\&q, p\&\neg p\}\perp p\&q = \{\varnothing\}$
f. $\{p\vee r, p\vee\neg r, q\&s, q\&\neg s\}\perp p\&q = \{\{p\vee r, p\vee\neg r\},\{p\vee r, q\&s\},\{p\vee r, q\&\neg s\},\{p\vee\neg r, q\&s\},\{p\vee\neg r, q\&\neg s\}\}$
g. $\{p\vee q, p\leftrightarrow q\}\perp p\&q = \{\{p\vee q\},\{p\leftrightarrow q\}\}$
h. $\{p\vee q, p\rightarrow q, q\rightarrow p\}\perp p\&q = \{\{p\vee q, p\rightarrow q\},\{p\vee q, q\rightarrow p\},\{p\rightarrow q, q\rightarrow p\}\}$
i. $\varnothing\perp p\&q = \{\varnothing\}$
j. $\varnothing\perp p\vee\neg p = \varnothing$
k. $\{p\&q\}\perp\{p,q\} = \{\varnothing\}$
l. $\{p\vee q\}\perp\{p,q\} = \{\{p\vee q\}\}$
m. $\{q,r\}\perp\{p,q\} = \{\{r\}\}$
n. $\{p\vee r,p\vee\neg r\}\perp\{p,q\} = \{\{p\vee r\},\{p\vee\neg r\}\}$
o. $\{p\vee q,p\rightarrow q,q\rightarrow p\}\perp\{p,q\} = \{\{p\vee q\},\{p\rightarrow q,q\rightarrow p\}\}$
p. $\{p,q,r\}\perp\varnothing = \{\{p,q,r\}\}$
q. $\{p,\neg p\}\perp\varnothing = \{\{p,\neg p\}\}$
r. $\{p,\neg p\}\perp\{r\} = \{\{p,\},\{\neg p\}\}$
s. $\varnothing\perp\varnothing = \{\varnothing\}$

27. Suppose not. It then follows from $\alpha \in \mathrm{Cn}(X)$ that $\alpha\vee\beta \in \mathrm{Cn}(X)$, contrary to $X \in A\perp(\alpha\vee\beta)$.

28. Let $X \in A\perp B_1 \cap A\perp B_2$. We are going to show that $X \in A\perp(B_1\cup B_2)$ by showing that the three conditions of Definition 1.35 are satisfied. We have $X \subseteq A$ from $X \in A\perp B_1$, so that (i) is satisfied. For (ii), suppose to the contrary that X implies some element of $B_1\cup B_2$. Then it either implies some element of B_1, contrary to $X \in A\perp B_1$, or some element of B_2, contrary to $X \in A\perp B_2$. We can conclude from this contradiction that (ii) is satisfied.

For (iii), suppose to the contrary that there is some Y such that $X \subset Y \subseteq A$ and $Y \cap \mathrm{Cn}(B_1\cup B_2) = \varnothing$. Then $Y \cap \mathrm{Cn}(B_1) = \varnothing$, contrary to $X \in A\perp B_1$. We may conclude from this contradiction that (iii) is also satisfied.

29. Let $X \in A\perp\alpha \cap A\perp\beta$. We are going to show that $X \in A\perp(\alpha\&\beta)$ by showing that the three conditions of Definition 1.35 are satisfied. We have $X \subseteq A$ from $X \in A\perp\alpha$, so that (i) is satisfied. For (ii), suppose to the contrary that $X \vdash \alpha\&\beta$. Then $X \vdash \alpha$, contrary to $X \in A\perp\alpha$. We can conclude from this contradiction that (ii) is satisfied.

For (iii), suppose to the contrary that there is some Y such that $X \subset Y \subseteq A$ and $\alpha\&\beta \notin \mathrm{Cn}(Y)$. Then either $\alpha \notin \mathrm{Cn}(Y)$, contrary to $X \in A\perp\alpha$, or $\beta \notin \mathrm{Cn}(Y)$, contrary to $X \in A\perp\beta$. We may conclude from this contradiction that (iii) is also satisfied.

30. Suppose to the contrary that $X \subset Y$. It follows from $Y \in A\perp\beta$ that $Y \nvdash \beta$, and then from $\vdash \alpha \rightarrow \beta$ that $Y \nvdash \alpha$. We therefore have $X \subset Y \subseteq A$, and $Y \nvdash \alpha$, contrary to $X \in A\perp\alpha$.

31. Suppose to the contrary that $\varnothing \in A\perp B$ and $\{\varnothing\} \neq A\perp B$. Then there is some X such that $\varnothing \neq X \in A\perp B$. But since $\varnothing \subset X$, $\varnothing$ and X cannot be elements of the same remainder set.

32. $\cup(X\perp Y)$ is a subset of X, and each element of $X \setminus \cup(X\perp Y)$ implies some element of Y. By repeated use of Observation 1.40, we obtain $X\perp Y = (\cup(X\perp Y))\perp Y$.

33. *Part I*: Suppose that $X \in (A\cup\{\alpha\})\perp\neg\alpha$. We are going to show (1) that $\alpha \in X$ and (2) that $X \in (A\cup\{\alpha\})\perp\perp$.

For (1), suppose to the contrary that $\alpha \notin X$. It follows from this and $X \in (A\cup\{\alpha\})\perp\neg\alpha$ that $X\cup\{\alpha\} \vdash \neg\alpha$. By deduction this yields $X \vdash \alpha \rightarrow \neg\alpha$, which is truth-functionally equivalent to $X \vdash \neg\alpha$. Since this contradicts $X \in (A\cup\{\alpha\})\perp\neg\alpha$, we may conclude that $\alpha \in X$.

For (2) we need to show that the three conditions of Definition 1.35 are satisfied. We already have $X \subseteq A\cup\{\alpha\}$, so that (i) is satisfied. For (ii), suppose to the contrary that $X \vdash \perp$. Then $X \vdash \neg\alpha$, contrary to $X \in (A\cup\{\alpha\})\perp\neg\alpha$. We may conclude from this contradiction that (ii) is satisfied.

For (iii), suppose to the contrary that there is some X' such that $X \subset X' \subseteq A\cup\{\alpha\}$ and $X' \nvdash \perp$. It follows from $\alpha \in X$ that $\alpha \in X'$. From this and $X' \nvdash \perp$ we may conclude that $X' \nvdash \neg\alpha$. We therefore have $X \subset X' \subseteq A\cup\{\alpha\}$ and $X' \nvdash \neg\alpha$, contrary to $X \in (A\cup\{\alpha\})\perp\neg\alpha$. From this contradiction, it can be concluded that (iii) holds.

Part II: Suppose that $\alpha \in X \in (A\cup\{\alpha\})\perp\perp$. We are going to show that $X \in (A\cup\{\alpha\})\perp\neg\alpha$, and as usual this amounts to showing that conditions (i)-(iii) of Definition 1.35 are satisfied. We already have $X \subseteq A\cup\{\alpha\}$, so that (i) is satisfied. For (ii), suppose to the contrary that $X \vdash \neg\alpha$. Since $\alpha \in X$, we then have $X \vdash \alpha\&\neg\alpha$, i.e., $X \vdash \perp$, contrary to $X \in (A\cup\{\alpha\})\perp\perp$. We can conclude that (ii) is satisfied. For (iii), suppose to the contrary that there is some Y such that $X \subset Y \subseteq A\cup\{\alpha\}$ and $Y \nvdash \neg\alpha$. Then $Y \nvdash \perp$, contrary to $X \in (A\cup\{\alpha\})\perp\perp$. The contradiction is sufficient to establish that (iii) holds, which concludes the proof.

34. Let $X \subseteq A\perp\beta$. It follows from Observation 1.40 that $A\perp\beta = A\perp\{\alpha,\beta\}$, so that $X \in A\perp\{\alpha,\beta\}$. It follows from this by Observation 1.44 that there is some Y such that $X \subseteq Y \in A\perp\alpha$.

35. If $A\perp\alpha = A\perp\beta$, then $X \not\subset Y \not\subset X$ for all $X \in A\perp\alpha$ and $Y \in A\perp\beta$. It follows from Observation 1.46 that $A\perp(\alpha\&\beta) = A\perp\alpha \cup A\perp\beta = A\perp\alpha$.

36. *For one direction*, let $X \in A\perp B$. Then $X \subseteq A$, and since X does not imply any element of B, $X \cap B = \varnothing$. It follows that $X \subseteq A \setminus B$, so that clause (i) of Definition 1.35 is satisfied. Since X implies no element of B, it implies no element of $\text{Cn}(A) \cap B$, and thus (ii) is satisfied.

To see that (iii) is satisfied, let $X \subset X' \subseteq A \setminus B$. Then since $X \in A\perp B$ there must be some $\beta \in B$ such that $X' \vdash \beta$. It follows from this and $X' \subseteq A$ that $\beta \in \text{Cn}(A)$, and consequently $\beta \in \text{Cn}(A) \cap B$. This shows that (iii) is satisfied.

For the other direction, let $X \in (A \setminus B)\perp(\text{Cn}(A) \cap B)$. It follows that $X \subseteq A$, so that clause (i) is satisfied. For (ii), suppose that X implies some element β of B. Then $\beta \in \text{Cn}(X)$ and, since $X \subseteq A$, $\beta \in \text{Cn}(A)$, so that $\beta \in \text{Cn}(A) \cap B$, contrary to $X \vdash \beta$ and $X \in (A \setminus B)\perp(\text{Cn}(A) \cap B)$. We can conclude from this contradiction that (ii) holds.

For (iii), let $\delta \in A \setminus X$. We need to show that $X \cup \{\delta\}$ implies some element of B. If $\delta \in B$, then this follows trivially. If $\delta \notin B$, then $X \subset X \cup \{\delta\} \subseteq A \setminus B$, and it follows from $X \in (A \setminus B)\perp(\text{Cn}(A) \cap B)$ that $X \cup \{\delta\}$ implies some element of $\text{Cn}(A) \cap B$. This is sufficient to show that (iii) holds.

37. a. Conditions (i') and (i) (of Definition 1.35) are the same. To show that (ii') and (ii) coincide for singletons, it is sufficient to note that $\{\beta\} \not\subseteq \text{Cn}(X)$ if and only if $\text{Cn}(X) \cap \{\beta\} = \varnothing$, by set theory. To see that (iii') and (iii) coincide, observe that $\{\beta\} \not\subseteq \text{Cn}(X')$ if and only if $\text{Cn}(X') \cap \{\beta\} = \varnothing$.
b. Let the language consist of the atomic sentences p and q and their truth-functional combinations. Let Cn be purely truth-functional. Then $\{p\} \in \{p,q\}\angle\{p,q\}$, but $\{p\} \notin \{p,q\}\perp\{p,q\}$.
c. Let $\beta = \&(B)$. We are going to show $A\angle B = A\perp\{\&(B)\}$ by proving first $A\angle B \subseteq A\perp\{\&(B)\}$ and then $A\perp\{\&(B)\} \subseteq A\angle B$.

Part I: Let $X \in A\angle B$. We are going to show that $X \in A\perp\{\&(B)\}$. This will be done by showing that the three conditions of Definition 1.35 are satisfied.

It follows from $X \in A\angle B$ that $X \subseteq A$, so that (i) is satisfied.

For (ii), suppose to the contrary that $\text{Cn}(X) \cap \{\&(B)\} \neq \varnothing$, i.e., that $\&(B) \in \text{Cn}(X)$. It follows that $B \subseteq \text{Cn}(X)$, contrary to $X \in A\angle B$. We may conclude that $\&(B) \notin \text{Cn}(X)$, so that (ii) is satisfied.

For (iii), suppose to the contrary that there is some X' such that $X \subset X' \subseteq A$ and $\&(B) \notin \text{Cn}(X')$. It follows that $B \not\subseteq \text{Cn}(X')$. We then have $X \subset X' \subseteq A$

and $B \not\subseteq \text{Cn}(X')$, contrary to $X \in A \angle B$. We can conclude from this contradiction that (iii) is satisfied.

Part II: Let $X \in A\perp\{\&(B)\}$. We are going to show that $X \in A\angle B$. To do this, we need to show that (i'), (ii'), and (iii') are satisfied.

It follows from $X \in A\perp\{\&(B)\}$ that $X \subseteq A$, so that (i') is satisfied.

For (ii'), suppose to the contrary that $B \subseteq \text{Cn}(X)$. Since $\&(B) \in \text{Cn}(B)$ we then have $\&(B) \in \text{Cn}(X)$, contrary to $X \in A\perp\{\&(B)\}$. We may conclude that $B \not\subseteq \text{Cn}(X)$, so that (ii') holds.

For (iii'), suppose to the contrary that there is some X' such that $X \subset X' \subseteq A$ and $B \not\subseteq \text{Cn}(X')$. It follows from $B \not\subseteq \text{Cn}(X')$ that $\&(B) \notin \text{Cn}(X')$. We then have $X \subset X' \subseteq A$ and $\&(B) \notin \text{Cn}(X')$, contrary to $X \in A\perp\{\&(B)\}$. We can conclude from this contradiction that (iii') is satisfied.

38. **a.** $A\perp(p\&q) = \{\{p, q\rightarrow p, p\vee q, \top\},\{p\leftrightarrow q, q\rightarrow p, p\rightarrow q, \top\},\{q, p\rightarrow q, p\vee q, \top\}\}$
b. $A\perp p = \{\{p\leftrightarrow q, q\rightarrow p, p\rightarrow q, \top\},\{q, p\rightarrow q, p\vee q, \top\}\}$
c. $A\perp(p\leftrightarrow q) = \{\{p, q\rightarrow p, p\vee q, \top\},\{q, p\rightarrow q, p\vee q, \top\}\}$
d. $A\perp(q\rightarrow p) = \{\{q, p\rightarrow q, p\vee q, \top\}\}$
e. $A\perp(p\vee q) = \{\{p\leftrightarrow q, q\rightarrow p, p\rightarrow q, \top\}\}$
f. $A\perp\{p,p\vee q\} = \{\{p\leftrightarrow q, q\rightarrow p, p\rightarrow q, \top\}\}$
g. $A\perp\{p,q\} = \{\{p\vee q,\top\},\{p\leftrightarrow q, p\rightarrow q, q\rightarrow p, \top\}\}$
h. $A\perp\{p\leftrightarrow q, p\vee q\} = \{\{q\rightarrow p,\top\},\{p\rightarrow q,\top\}\}$
i. $A\perp\{p,q,p\leftrightarrow q\} = \{\{q\rightarrow p,\top\},\{p\rightarrow q,\top\},\{p\vee q,\top\}\}$

39. It follows from Observation 1.56 that $A\perp(\alpha\vee\beta) = A\perp\alpha \cap A\perp\beta$. We have $A\perp\alpha \cap A\perp\beta \subseteq A\perp\alpha \cup A\perp\beta$, and from Observation 1.55 we obtain $A\perp\alpha \cup A\perp\beta = A\perp(\alpha\&\beta)$.

40. It follows from $X \subseteq A$ and $\alpha \in A$, by the logical closure of A, that $\text{Cn}(X\cup\{\alpha\}) \subseteq A$. For the other direction, we need to show that if $\beta \in A$, then $\beta \in \text{Cn}(X\cup\{\alpha\})$. Let $\beta \in A$. It follows from the corollary of Observation 1.52 (the recovery lemma) that $\alpha\rightarrow\beta \in X$. By deduction, $\beta \in \text{Cn}(X\cup\{\alpha\})$.

41. It follows from Observation 1.52 (the recovery lemma) that $\alpha\rightarrow\beta \in \text{Cn}(X)$, which is equivalent to $\neg\beta\rightarrow\neg\alpha \in \text{Cn}(X)$. The deduction property yields $\neg\alpha \in \text{Cn}(X\cup\{\neg\beta\})$, from which follows $\text{Cn}(X\cup\{\neg\alpha\}) \subseteq \text{Cn}(X\cup\{\neg\beta\})$.

42. Let $\beta \in Y\backslash X$. Then $\beta \in A\backslash X$. It follows from Observation 1.53 that $X \in A\perp\beta$ and from the corollary of Observation 1.52 that $\text{Cn}(X\cup\{\beta\}) = A$. Since $X\cup\{\beta\} \subseteq Y$, we therefore have $Y\subset A = \text{Cn}(X\cup\{\beta\}) \subseteq \text{Cn}(Y)$, so that $Y\subset\text{Cn}(Y)$.

43. It follows from the logical closure of X that if $\beta \in X$ then $\alpha\vee\beta \in X$.

For the other direction, suppose to the contrary that $\alpha\vee\beta \in X$ and $\beta \notin X$. It follows from $\beta \in A\backslash X$ and $X \in A\perp\alpha$ that $X\cup\{\beta\} \vdash \alpha$. Since X is logically closed, we have $\beta\rightarrow\alpha \in X$. Since $\alpha\vee\beta$ and $\beta\rightarrow\alpha$ together imply α, it follows from $\alpha\vee\beta \in X$ and $\beta\rightarrow\alpha \in X$ that $X \vdash \alpha$, contrary to $X \in A\perp\alpha$. This contradiction concludes the proof.

44. *Part I*: We are first going to show that if $X \in A\perp\alpha$, then $\alpha \notin X \in A\perp\kappa$. It follows from $X \in A\perp\alpha$ that $\alpha \notin X$. We are going to show that $X \in A\perp\kappa$.

Since $\alpha \in A$ it follows from $X \in A\perp\alpha$ that $X \subset A$, so that $\kappa \notin X$. We now have $X \in A\perp\alpha$ and $\kappa \in A\backslash X$. It follows from Observation 1.53 that $X \in A\perp\kappa$.

Part II: For the other direction of the observation, suppose that $\alpha \notin X \in A\perp\kappa$. We then have $\alpha \in A\backslash X$, and $X \in A\perp\alpha$ follows directly from Observation 1.53.

45. Let $X \in A\perp\alpha$, and $\beta \in A$. In order to prove that $\alpha\rightarrow\beta \in X$, suppose to the contrary that $\alpha\rightarrow\beta \notin X$.

It follows from $\beta \in A$, by the logical closure of A, that $\alpha\rightarrow\beta \in A$. We therefore have $\alpha\rightarrow\beta \in A\backslash X$. Since $X \in A\perp\alpha$, it follows that $X\cup\{\alpha\rightarrow\beta\} \vdash \alpha$. By the deduction property, this is equivalent with $X \vdash (\alpha\rightarrow\beta)\rightarrow\alpha$, which is truth-functionally equivalent with $X \vdash \alpha$. This, however contradicts our assumption that $X \in A\perp\alpha$. We may conclude from this contradiction that $\alpha\rightarrow\beta \in X$.

46. Suppose to the contrary that $B_1 \subset B_2$, $B_1 \in A\perp\alpha$, and $B_2 \in A\perp\beta$. From Observation 1.55 we have $B_1 \subset B_2$, $B_1 \in A\perp\alpha\&\beta$, and $B_2 \in A\perp\alpha\&\beta$, which is impossible since an element of a remainder set cannot be a proper subset of another element of that same remainder set.

47. If B is logically closed, then $B\cap\text{Cn}(\varnothing) \neq \varnothing$, and it follows by monotony that $B\cap\text{Cn}(X) \neq \varnothing$ for all sets of sentences. It follows from Definition 1.35, clause (ii), that $A\perp B$ is empty.

48. Since $\alpha\leftrightarrow\beta$ is equivalent to $(\alpha\&\beta)\vee(\neg\alpha\&\neg\beta)$, this follows directly from Part 3 of Observation 1.57.

49. $[\alpha] = \{X \mid \alpha \in X \in \mathcal{L}\perp\perp\}$, by Observation 1.58 $= \{X \mid X \in \mathcal{L}\perp\neg\alpha\} = \mathcal{L}\perp\neg\alpha$.

50. Since $A\cap X \subseteq X$, clause (i) of Definition 1.35 is satisfied. Since $X \nvdash \alpha$, $A\cap X \nvdash \alpha$, so that clause (ii) is satisfied.

In order to show that clause (iii) is satisfied, suppose to the contrary that there is some $\beta \in A \setminus (A \cap X)$ such that $(A \cap X) \cup \{\beta\} \nvdash \alpha$. Then $\beta \rightarrow \alpha \notin A \cap X$. Since both α and β are elements of A, so is $\beta \rightarrow \alpha$, and we may conclude that $\beta \rightarrow \alpha \notin X$. Since $X \in \mathcal{L} \perp \perp$, it follows that $\neg(\beta \rightarrow \alpha) \in X$. Furthermore, it follows from $\beta \in A \setminus (A \cap X)$ that $\beta \notin X$, hence $\neg\beta \in X$. We now have $\{\neg\beta, \neg(\beta \rightarrow \alpha)\} \subseteq X$, which is impossible since it requires X to be inconsistent.

51. Let $B = \{\beta_1, \ldots \beta_n\}$. Then:
$X \in [B]$
iff $B \subseteq X \in \mathcal{L} \perp \perp$ (Definition 1.59)
iff $\beta_k \in X \in \mathcal{L} \perp \perp$ for all $1 \leq k \leq n$
iff $X \in \mathcal{L} \perp \neg\beta_k$ for all $1 \leq k \leq n$ (Observation 1.58)
iff $X \in (\mathcal{L} \perp \neg\beta_1) \cap \ldots \cap (\mathcal{L} \perp \neg\beta_n)$
iff $X \in \mathcal{L} \perp (\neg\beta_1 \vee \ldots \vee \neg\beta_n)$ (Observation 1.56)
iff $X \in \mathcal{L} \perp n(B)$.

52. a. $[\alpha] \subseteq [\beta]$
iff $[\mathrm{Cn}(\{\alpha\})] \subseteq [\mathrm{Cn}(\{\beta\})]$
iff $\mathrm{Cn}(\{\beta\}) \subseteq \mathrm{Cn}(\{\alpha\})$ (Observation 1.61)
iff $\vdash \alpha \rightarrow \beta$.
b. $[\neg\alpha]$
$= \{X \mid \neg\alpha \in X \in \mathcal{L} \perp \perp\}$
$= (\mathcal{L} \perp \perp) \setminus \{X \mid \neg\alpha \notin X \in \mathcal{L} \perp \perp\}$
$= (\mathcal{L} \perp \perp) \setminus \{X \mid \alpha \in X \in \mathcal{L} \perp \perp\}$ (Observation 1.57)
$= (\mathcal{L} \perp \perp) \setminus [\alpha]$.
c. $[\alpha \& \beta]$
$= [\{\alpha, \beta\}]$
$= [\{\alpha\}] \cap [\{\beta\}]$ (Observation 1.61)
$= [\alpha] \cap [\beta]$
d. $[\alpha \vee \beta]$
$= \{X \mid \alpha \vee \beta \in X \in \mathcal{L} \perp \perp\}$
$= \{X \mid (\alpha \in X \in \mathcal{L} \perp \perp) \vee (\beta \in X \in \mathcal{L} \perp \perp)\}$ (Observation 1.57, Part 3)
$= \{X \mid \alpha \in X \in \mathcal{L} \perp \perp\} \cup \{X \mid \beta \in X \in \mathcal{L} \perp \perp\}$
$= [\alpha] \cup [\beta]$.
e. $[\alpha \rightarrow \beta]$
$= [\neg\alpha \vee \beta]$
$= [\neg\alpha] \cup [\beta]$ (Part *d* of this exercise)
$= ((\mathcal{L} \perp \perp) \setminus [\alpha]) \cup [\beta]$ (Part *b* of this exercise)
$= (\mathcal{L} \perp \perp) \setminus ([\alpha] \setminus [\beta])$

53. a. $X \in A \perp (\alpha \& \beta)$
iff $g_A(X) \in \mathcal{L} \perp (\alpha \& \beta)$

iff $\neg(\alpha\&\beta) \in g_A(X)$
iff $\neg\alpha\vee\neg\beta \in g_A(X)$
iff $\neg\alpha \in g_A(X)$ or $\neg\beta \in g_A(X)$ (Observation 1.57, Part 3)
iff $\alpha \notin g_A(X)$ or $\beta \notin g_A(X)$ (Observation 1.57, Part 2)
iff $g_A(X) \in \mathcal{L}\bot\alpha$ or $g_A(X) \in \mathcal{L}\bot\beta$
iff $X \in A\bot\alpha$ or $X \in A\bot\beta$
iff $X \in (A\bot\alpha \cup A\bot\beta)$
b. $X \in A\bot(\alpha\vee\beta)$
iff $g_A(X) \in \mathcal{L}\bot(\alpha\vee\beta)$
iff $\neg(\alpha\vee\beta) \in g_A(X)$
iff $\neg\alpha\&\neg\beta \in g_A(X)$
iff $\neg\alpha \in g_A(X)$ and $\neg\beta \in g_A(X)$
iff $\alpha \notin g_A(X)$ and $\beta \notin g_A(X)$ (Observation 1.57, Part 2)
iff $g_A(X) \in \mathcal{L}\bot\alpha$ and $g_A(X) \in \mathcal{L}\bot\beta$
iff $X \in A\bot\alpha$ and $X \in A\bot\beta$
iff $X \in (A\bot\alpha \cap A\bot\beta)$

54. No. Let $A = \{\delta,\neg\delta\}$.

55. Let $B = \{\beta_1,\ldots \beta_n\}$. Then
$A\Delta B = A\bot\beta_1 \cup\ldots\cup A\bot\beta_n$
$= A\bot(\beta_1\&\ldots\&\beta_n)$ (Observation 1.55)
$= A\bot(\&B)$.

56. Let $B = \{\beta_1,\ldots\beta_n\}$. Then $A\Delta B = A\Delta\{\beta_1,\ldots\beta_n\} = (A\bot\beta_1) \cup\ldots\cup (A\bot\beta_n)$.

For each $\beta_k \in B$ it follows from $A\bot\beta_k \subseteq A\Delta D$, according to Observation 1.66, that there is some finite subset D_k of D such that $A\bot\beta_1 \subseteq A\Delta D_k$. It follows that
$(A\bot\beta_1) \cup\ldots\cup (A\bot\beta_n) \subseteq (A\Delta D_1) \cup\ldots\cup (A\Delta D_k)$, thus
$A\Delta B \subseteq (A\Delta(D_1\cup\ldots\cup D_k))$.
Let $D' = D_1\cup\ldots\cup D_k$. Then D' is a finite subset of D, and $A\Delta B \subseteq A\Delta D$, as desired.

57. Both equations can be solved if and only if $\text{Cn}(A)\cap B = \varnothing$, and $X = A$ is then a solution.

58. Both equations have a trivial solution for all sets A, since $A\bot\varnothing = \{A\}$ for all A.

59. Clearly, (a) implies (b). In order to see that (b) implies (a), suppose that $\{A_1,\ldots A_n\} = X\bot Y$. Then $A_1\cup\ldots\cup A_n \subseteq X$.

It follows from the upper bound property that each element of $X \setminus \cup(X \perp Y)$ implies some element of Y. It follows from Observation 1.40 that $X \perp Y = (\cup(X \perp Y)) \perp Y$. Furthermore, $(\cup(X \perp Y)) \perp Y = (A_1 \cup \ldots \cup A_n) \perp Y$, and we are done.

60. The condition is that A and B are mutually closed and that $A \not\subset B \not\subset A$. (Cf. Exercise 24 for the definition of mutual closure.)

Proof that this condition is necessary: Let $\{A,B\} \subseteq X \perp Y$. Then clearly $A \not\subset B \not\subset A$. Suppose that A and B are not mutually closed. Then either A is not B-closed, or B is not A-closed. Without loss of generality, we may assume that A is not B-closed. Since $B \subseteq X$ it follows from Observation 1.29 that A is not X-closed. According to Observation 1.36, this contradicts $A \in X \perp Y$. We may conclude that A and B are mutually closed.

Proof that the condition is sufficient: Suppose that A and B are mutually closed and that $A \not\subset B \not\subset A$. Since A is A-closed, it follows from its B-closure by Observation 1.29 that A is $A \cup B$-closed. Similarly, B is $A \cup B$-closed. The rest follows from Observation 1.68.

61. It follows from Observation 1.70 that there are sentences α_1' and α_2' such that $\{A_1\} = B \perp \alpha_1'$ and $\{A_2\} = B \perp \alpha_2'$. Furthermore, it follows from Observation 1.46 that $\{A_1, A_2\} = B \perp (\alpha_1' \& \alpha_2')$.

62. Given the Corollary of Observation 1.70, it remains to show that $\{A\} = B \perp (\alpha \vee \bigvee(B \setminus A))$. There are two cases, according to whether or not $B \setminus A = \varnothing$.

Case 1, $B \setminus A = \varnothing$: Then $\bigvee(B \setminus A) = \perp$ and $\vdash \alpha \vee \bigvee(B \setminus A) \leftrightarrow \alpha$. We therefore have $A \in B \perp (\alpha \vee \bigvee(B \setminus A))$ directly from $A \in B \perp \alpha$. It follows from $B \setminus A = \varnothing$ and $A \in B \perp \alpha$ that $A = B$. We may conclude that $\{A\} = B \perp (\alpha \vee \bigvee(B \setminus A)$, as desired.

Case 2, $B \setminus A \neq \varnothing$: Let $B \setminus A = \{\xi_1, \ldots \xi_n\}$. Then $\alpha \vee \bigvee(B \setminus A) = (\alpha \vee \xi_1 \vee \ldots \vee \xi_n)$. We are first going to show that $A \in B \perp (\alpha \vee \xi_1 \vee \ldots \vee \xi_n)$. Again, this will be done by showing that the three conditions of Definition 1.35 are satisfied.

It follows from $A \in B \perp \alpha$ that $A \subseteq B$, so that (i) is satisfied.

In order to prove (ii), we make use of $A \in B \perp \alpha$ to conclude that for each ξ_k, $A \cup \{\xi_k\} \vdash \alpha$ and, by the deduction property, $A \vdash \xi_k \rightarrow \alpha$. Now suppose that (ii) is not satisfied. Then $A \vdash (\alpha \vee \xi_1 \vee \ldots \vee \xi_n)$. Since $A \vdash \xi_k \rightarrow \alpha$ holds for every ξ_k, it would follow truth-functionally that $A \vdash \alpha$, contrary to $A \in B \perp \alpha$. We can conclude from this contradiction that $A \nvdash (\alpha \vee \xi_1 \vee \ldots \vee \xi_n)$, i.e., that (ii) is satisfied.

For (iii), suppose to the contrary that there is some set X such that $A \subset X \subseteq B$ and $X \nvdash (\alpha \vee \xi_1 \vee \ldots \vee \xi_n)$. It follows set-theoretically from $A \subset X \subseteq B$ that there is some $\xi_k \in B \setminus A$ such that $\xi_k \in X$. Since $\xi_k \vdash (\alpha \vee \xi_1 \vee \ldots \vee \xi_n)$ we obtain

$X \vdash (\alpha \vee \xi_1 \vee ... \vee \xi_n)$, contrary to our assumption. This contradiction is sufficient to show that (iii) is satisfied.

We have now proved that $A \in B \perp (\alpha \vee \xi_1 \vee ... \vee \xi_n)$. It remains to be shown that $\{A\} = B \perp (\alpha \vee \xi_1 \vee ... \vee \xi_n)$. For that purpose, let $W \in B \perp (\alpha \vee \xi_1 \vee ... \vee \xi_n)$. Our task is to show that $W = A$.

Since all elements of $B \setminus A$ imply $\alpha \vee \xi_1 \vee ... \vee \xi_n$, it follows from $W \in B \perp (\alpha \vee \xi_1 \vee ... \vee \xi_n)$ that $W \cap (B \setminus A) = \varnothing$. Since A and W are subsets of B, it follows set-theoretically that $W \subseteq A$. Since A and W are elements of the same remainder set, we have $W \not\subset A$, and consequently $W = A$. This concludes the proof.

SOLUTIONS FOR CHAPTER 2^+

63. a. By *recovery*, $A \subseteq \text{Cn}((A+(\alpha\vee\beta))\cup\{\alpha\vee\beta\})$. Since $\alpha \in A$, it follows that $\alpha \in \text{Cn}((A+(\alpha\vee\beta))\cup\{\alpha\vee\beta\})$. By the deduction property of Cn, this is equivalent to $(\alpha\vee\beta)\rightarrow\alpha \in \text{Cn}(A+(\alpha\vee\beta))$, i.e., $\beta\rightarrow\alpha \in \text{Cn}(A+(\alpha\vee\beta))$. By *closure*, this is equivalent to $\beta\rightarrow\alpha \in A+(\alpha\vee\beta)$.
b. It follows from *recovery* and $\alpha \in A$ that $\alpha \in \text{Cn}((A+(\alpha\rightarrow\beta))\cup\{\alpha\rightarrow\beta\})$, thus by the deduction propety, $(\alpha\rightarrow\beta)\rightarrow\alpha \in \text{Cn}(A+(\alpha\rightarrow\beta))$, or equivalently $\alpha \in \text{Cn}(A+(\alpha\rightarrow\beta))$. It follows from *closure* that $\alpha \in A+(\alpha\rightarrow\beta)$.

64. Let $\vdash \alpha$. We need to show that $A+\alpha = A$. It follows from *inclusion* that $A+\alpha \subseteq A$. It remains to be shown that $A \subseteq A+\alpha$.

Let $\varepsilon \in A$. By *recovery*, $A \subseteq \text{Cn}((A+\alpha)\cup\{\alpha\})$, so that $\varepsilon \in \text{Cn}((A+\alpha)\cup\{\alpha\})$. By the deduction property of Cn, $\alpha\rightarrow\varepsilon \in \text{Cn}(A+\alpha)$. It follows from $\vdash \alpha$ that $\alpha\rightarrow\varepsilon$ is logically equivalent to ε, and we therefore have $\varepsilon \in \text{Cn}(A+\alpha)$. It follows by *relative closure* from $\varepsilon \in A$ and $\varepsilon \in \text{Cn}(A+\alpha)$ that $\varepsilon \in A+\alpha$. This concludes the proof.

65. Suppose that $\beta \in A+\alpha$. Then $\alpha\vee\beta \in A+\alpha$ follows from *closure*. For the other direction, let $\alpha\vee\beta \in A+\alpha$. Since $\beta \in A$ it follows from *recovery* that $\alpha\rightarrow\beta \in \text{Cn}(A+\alpha)$. Since $\alpha\vee\beta$ and $\alpha\rightarrow\beta$ together imply β, it follows that $\beta \in \text{Cn}(A+\alpha)$, and we can use *closure* to obtain $\beta \in A+\alpha$.

66. a. Let $\delta \in A$ and $\delta \in \text{Cn}(\{\neg\alpha\})$. It follows from $\delta \in \text{Cn}(\{\neg\alpha\})$ that $\vdash\neg\alpha\rightarrow\delta$. It follows by *recovery* from $\delta \in A$ that $\alpha\rightarrow\delta \in \text{Cn}(A+\alpha)$. Since δ follows from $\neg\alpha\rightarrow\delta$ and $\alpha\rightarrow\delta$, we may conclude that $\delta \in \text{Cn}(A+\alpha)$.
b. From Part *a* and Observation 2.12.

67. Suppose to the contrary that $\alpha_1 \notin A+(\alpha_1\&\alpha_2)$, $\alpha_2 \notin A+(\alpha_1\&\alpha_2)$, and $\alpha_1\leftrightarrow\alpha_2 \notin A+(\alpha_1\&\alpha_2)$. It follows by *fullness* from $\alpha_1 \in A$ and $\alpha_1 \notin A+(\alpha_1\&\alpha_2)$ that $\alpha_1\&\alpha_2 \in \text{Cn}(((A+(\alpha_1\&\alpha_2))\cup\{\alpha_1\})$. It follows by the deduction property of Cn that $(\alpha_1 \rightarrow \alpha_1\&\alpha_2) \in \text{Cn}((A+(\alpha_1\&\alpha_2))$. In the same way (substitute α_2 for α_1) it follows that $(\alpha_2 \rightarrow \alpha_1\&\alpha_2) \in \text{Cn}((A+(\alpha_1\&\alpha_2))$, and (substitute $\alpha_1\leftrightarrow\alpha_2$ for α_1) that $(\alpha_1\leftrightarrow\alpha_2 \rightarrow \alpha_1\&\alpha_2) \in \text{Cn}((A+(\alpha_1\&\alpha_2))$.

In summary, we have shown that $\alpha_1 \rightarrow \alpha_1\&\alpha_2$, $\alpha_2 \rightarrow \alpha_1\&\alpha_2$ and $(\alpha_1\leftrightarrow\alpha_2) \rightarrow \alpha_1\&\alpha_2$ are all elements of $\text{Cn}((A+(\alpha_1\&\alpha_2))$. Together, these three expressions imply $\alpha_1\&\alpha_2$, and we may conclude that $\alpha_1\&\alpha_2 \in \text{Cn}((A+(\alpha_1\&\alpha_2))$. It follows from *success* that $\alpha_1\&\alpha_2 \in \text{Cn}(\varnothing)$. However, it follows by *closure* from $\alpha_1 \notin A+(\alpha_1\&\alpha_2)$ that $\alpha_1 \notin \text{Cn}(\varnothing)$, and thus $\alpha_1\&\alpha_2 \notin \text{Cn}(\varnothing)$. This contradiction concludes the proof.

68. Suppose to the contrary that there is some α such that $\alpha \in A$ and $\alpha \notin A+\neg\alpha$. It follows from *core-retainment* that there is some set A' such that $A' \subseteq A$, $\neg\alpha \notin \mathrm{Cn}(A')$ and $\neg\alpha \in \mathrm{Cn}(A' \cup \{\alpha\})$. However, $\neg\alpha \in \mathrm{Cn}(A' \cup \{\alpha\})$ implies $\alpha \rightarrow \neg\alpha \in \mathrm{Cn}(A')$ and thus $\neg\alpha \in \mathrm{Cn}(A')$.

69. a. *(i) implies (ii)*: Let X be such that $X \subseteq A$, $X \nvdash \alpha$ and $X \cup \{\beta\} \vdash \alpha$. It follows from the upper bound property that there is some X' such that $X \subseteq X' \in A \perp \alpha$ To see that (ii) is satisfied, it is sufficient to note that $\beta \notin X'$ follows from $X \subseteq X'$, $X' \nvdash \alpha$ and $X \cup \{\beta\} \vdash \alpha$.

(ii) implies (i): Let X be such that $\beta \notin X \in A \perp \alpha$. Then we directly have $X \subseteq A$ and $X \nvdash \alpha$. Since $\beta \in A$, but $\beta \notin X \in A \perp \alpha$, it follows from the maximality of remainders that $X \cup \{\beta\} \vdash \alpha$.

b. Core-retainment has been defined as follows:

(1) If $\beta \in A$ and $\beta \notin A+\alpha$, then there is a set A' such that $A' \subseteq A$ and that $\alpha \notin \mathrm{Cn}(A')$ but $\alpha \in \mathrm{Cn}(A' \cup \{\beta\})$.

By Part *a*, this is equivalent to:

(2) If $\beta \in A$ and $\beta \notin A+\alpha$, then there is some X such that $\beta \notin X \in A \perp \alpha$.

This is equivalent to:

(3) If $\beta \in A$ and $\beta \notin A+\alpha$, then $A \perp \alpha$ is non-empty and $\beta \notin \cap(A \perp \alpha)$.

Since α is not logically true, $A \perp \alpha$ is non-empty, and (3) is equivalent to:

(4) If $\beta \in A$ and $\beta \notin A+\alpha$, then $\beta \notin \cap(A \perp \alpha)$.

If $\beta \notin A$, then β is not included in any element of $A \perp \alpha$. Therefore, we can simplify (4) as follows:

(5) If $\beta \notin A+\alpha$, then $\beta \notin \cap(A \perp \alpha)$.

(6) $\cap(A \perp \alpha) \subseteq A+\alpha$.

70. a. *(i) implies (ii)*: Let X be such that $B \subseteq X \subseteq A$, $X \nvdash \alpha$ and $X \cup \{\beta\} \vdash \alpha$. It follows from the upper bound property that there is some X' such that $X \subseteq X' \in A \perp \alpha$. To see that (ii) is satisfied, it is sufficient to note that $B \subseteq X' \in A \perp \alpha$ and that $\beta \notin X'$. (The latter can be concluded from $X \subseteq X'$, $X' \nvdash \alpha$ and $X \cup \{\beta\} \vdash \alpha$.)

(ii) implies (i): Let X be such that $B \subseteq X \in A \perp \alpha$ and $\beta \notin X$. Then we directly have $B \subseteq X \subseteq A$ and $X \nvdash \alpha$. Since $\beta \in A$, but $\beta \notin X \in A \perp \alpha$, it follows from the maximality of remainders that $X \cup \{\beta\} \vdash \alpha$.

b. Relevance has been defined as follows:

(1) If $\beta \in A$ and $\beta \notin A+\alpha$, then there is a set A' such that $A+\alpha \subseteq A' \subseteq A$ and that $\alpha \notin \mathrm{Cn}(A')$ but $\alpha \in \mathrm{Cn}(A' \cup \{\beta\})$.

By Part *a*, this is equivalent to:

(2) If $\beta \in A$ and $\beta \notin A+\alpha$, then there is some X such that $A+\alpha \subseteq X \in A \perp \alpha$ and $\beta \notin X$.

This is equivalent to:

(3) If $\beta \in A$ and $\beta \notin A+\alpha$, then $\{X \mid A+\alpha \subseteq X \in A\bot\alpha\}$ is non-empty and $\beta \notin \cap\{X \mid A+\alpha \subseteq X \in A\bot\alpha\}$

Since *success* is satisfied and α is not logically true, $\{X \mid A+\alpha \subseteq X \in A\bot\alpha\}$ is non-empty, and (3) is equivalent to:

(4) If $\beta \in A$ and $\beta \notin A+\alpha$, then $\beta \notin \cap\{X \mid A+\alpha \subseteq X \in A\bot\alpha\}$

If $\beta \notin A$, then β is not included in any element of $A\bot\alpha$. Therefore, we can simplify (4) as follows:

(5) If $\beta \notin A+\alpha$, then $\beta \notin \cap\{X \mid A+\alpha \subseteq X \in A\bot\alpha\}$

(6) $\cap\{X \mid A+\alpha \subseteq X \in A\bot\alpha\} \subseteq A+\alpha$

Finally, since each element of $\{X \mid A+\alpha \subseteq X \in A\bot\alpha\}$ contains $A+\alpha$, (6) is equivalent to:

(7) $A+\alpha = \cap\{X \mid A+\alpha \subseteq X \in A\bot\alpha\}$.

71. a. If $\alpha \notin \text{Cn}(\varnothing)$ and $AC_{\alpha}B$, then $\alpha \notin \text{Cn}(B)$.

b. If $AC_{\alpha}B$, then $B \subseteq A$.

c. If $\alpha \leftrightarrow \beta \in \text{Cn}(\varnothing)$, then it holds for all sets B that $AC_{\alpha}B$ if and only if $AC_{\beta}B$.

72. Suppose that $\delta \in A+\alpha$. It follows from *closure* that $\alpha \vee \delta \in A+\alpha$. We also have $\alpha \vee \delta \in \text{Cn}(\{\alpha\})$. By *partial antitony*, $(A+\alpha) \cap \text{Cn}(\{\alpha\}) \subseteq A+(\alpha\&\beta)$, from which we can conclude that $\alpha \vee \delta \in A+(\alpha\&\beta)$.

73. a. Let + be an operation for A that satisfies *success*, *failure*, and *conjunctive inclusion*.

In the limiting case when $\vdash \alpha\&\beta$, we also have $\vdash \alpha$, and it follows from *failure* that $A+(\alpha\&\beta) = A = A+\alpha$, so that conjunctive covering holds.

In the principal case, when $\nvdash \alpha\&\beta$, it follows from *success* that $\alpha\&\beta \notin \text{Cn}(A+(\alpha\&\beta))$. From this we may conclude that either $\alpha \notin \text{Cn}(A+(\alpha\&\beta))$ or $\beta \notin \text{Cn}(A+(\alpha\&\beta))$. It follows from this, by *conjunctive inclusion*, that either $A+(\alpha\&\beta) \subseteq A+\alpha$ or $A+(\alpha\&\beta) \subseteq A+\beta$, so that *conjunctive covering* holds.

b. By set theory from Part *a*.

c. Let $\alpha \notin A+\beta$. It follows from Part *a* that either $A+(\alpha\&\beta) \subseteq A+\alpha$ or $A+(\alpha\&\beta) \subseteq A+\beta$. We need to show that if $A+(\alpha\&\beta) \subseteq A+\beta$, then $A+(\alpha\&\beta) \subseteq A+\alpha$.

It follows from $A+(\alpha\&\beta) \subseteq A+\beta$ and $\alpha \notin A+\beta$ that $\alpha \notin A+(\alpha\&\beta)$. From this it follows, since *closure* is satisfied, that $\alpha \notin \text{Cn}(A+(\alpha\&\beta))$. We can use *conjunctive inclusion* to conclude that $A+(\alpha\&\beta) \subseteq A+\alpha$.

74. Let A be logically closed, and let + be an operator for A that satisfies *closure*, *inclusion*, *extensionality*, *recovery*, and *conjunctive overlap*. In order to show that *conjunctive trisection* holds, let $\alpha \in A+(\alpha\&\beta)$. We are going to show that $\alpha \in A+(\alpha\&\beta\&\delta)$.

Since $\alpha\&\beta\&\delta$ is logically equivalent to $(\alpha\&\beta)\&(\alpha\&\beta\rightarrow\delta)$, it follows from *extensionality* that we can solve our task by proving that $\alpha \in A+((\alpha\&\beta)\&(\alpha\&\beta\rightarrow\delta))$. If we can prove both $\alpha \in A+(\alpha\&\beta)$ and $\alpha \in A+(\alpha\&\beta\rightarrow\delta)$, then $\alpha \in A+((\alpha\&\beta)\&(\alpha\&\beta\rightarrow\delta))$ will follow directly from *conjunctive overlap*. Since $\alpha \in A+(\alpha\&\beta)$ was one of our assumptions, it only remains to show that $\alpha \in A+(\alpha\&\beta\rightarrow\delta)$.

This can be proved from *recovery*. It follows from *recovery* that $A \subseteq \mathrm{Cn}((A+(\alpha\&\beta\rightarrow\delta))\cup\{\alpha\&\beta\rightarrow\delta\})$. It follows from $\alpha \in A+(\alpha\&\beta)$, by *inclusion*, that $\alpha \in A$. We therefore have $(A+(\alpha\&\beta\rightarrow\delta))\cup\{\alpha\&\beta\rightarrow\delta\} \vdash \alpha$. By the deduction property of Cn, we then have $A+(\alpha\&\beta\rightarrow\delta) \vdash ((\alpha\&\beta\rightarrow\delta)\rightarrow\alpha)$. Since $(\alpha\&\beta\rightarrow\delta)\rightarrow\alpha$ is truth-functionally equivalent to α, we then have $A+(\alpha\&\beta\rightarrow\delta) \vdash \alpha$. By *closure*, $\alpha \in A+(\alpha\&\beta\rightarrow\delta)$, as desired.

75. a. Let $\beta \in A+(\alpha\&\beta)$. We are going to show that $A+(\alpha\&\beta) \subseteq A+\alpha$. There are two cases, according to whether or not $\alpha\&\beta$ is logically true.

Case 1, $\vdash\alpha\&\beta$: It follows that $\vdash\alpha$, and by *failure* that $A+(\alpha\&\beta) = A$ and $A+\alpha = A$. From this, $A+(\alpha\&\beta) \subseteq A+\alpha$ follows directly.

Case 2, $\nvdash \alpha\&\beta$: It follows from *success* that $\alpha\&\beta \notin \mathrm{Cn}(A+(\alpha\&\beta))$. From this and $\beta \in A+(\alpha\&\beta)$ we can conclude that $\alpha \notin \mathrm{Cn}(A+(\alpha\&\beta))$. It follows from *conjunctive inclusion* that $A+(\alpha\&\beta) \subseteq A+\alpha$.

b. Let $\beta \in A+(\alpha\&\beta)$. In order to show that $A+\alpha \subseteq A+(\alpha\&\beta)$, let $\varepsilon \in A+\alpha$. Our task is to show that $\varepsilon \in A+(\alpha\&\beta)$. Since $\beta \in A+(\alpha\&\beta)$ and $A+(\alpha\&\beta)$ is logically closed (by *closure*) it is sufficient to show that $\beta\rightarrow\varepsilon \in A+(\alpha\&\beta)$.

It follows from $\varepsilon \in A+\alpha$ by *inclusion* that $\varepsilon \in A$. By *recovery*, $A \subseteq \mathrm{Cn}((A+\beta)\cup\{\beta\})$. It follows from the deduction property of Cn that $\beta\rightarrow\varepsilon \in \mathrm{Cn}(A+\beta)$, and from *closure* that $\beta\rightarrow\varepsilon \in A+\beta$.

Since $\beta\rightarrow\varepsilon$ is a logical consequence of ε it also follows by *closure*, from $\varepsilon \in A+\alpha$, that $\beta\rightarrow\varepsilon \in A+\alpha$. We therefore have $\beta\rightarrow\varepsilon \in (A+\alpha)\cap(A+\beta)$. By *conjunctive overlap*, $\beta\rightarrow\varepsilon \in A+(\alpha\&\beta)$. Since we have assumed that $\beta \in A+(\alpha\&\beta)$, it follows that $\varepsilon \in \mathrm{Cn}(A+(\alpha\&\beta))$. By *closure*, $\varepsilon \in A+(\alpha\&\beta)$, which finishes our proof.

c. Let $\alpha\rightarrow\beta \in A+\beta$. Then it follows from *extensionality* that $\alpha\rightarrow\beta \in A+((\alpha\rightarrow\beta)\&(\alpha\vee\beta))$. It follows from (1) that $A+((\alpha\rightarrow\beta)\&(\alpha\vee\beta)) \subseteq A+(\alpha\vee\beta)$, thus by *extensionality* that $A+\beta \subseteq A+(\alpha\vee\beta)$. Furthermore, it follows from $\alpha\rightarrow\beta \in A+((\alpha\rightarrow\beta)\&(\alpha\vee\beta))$ by (2) that $A+(\alpha\vee\beta) \subseteq A+((\alpha\rightarrow\beta)\&(\alpha\vee\beta))$, and thus by *extensionality* that $A+(\alpha\vee\beta) \subseteq A+\beta$. We can conclude that $A+\beta = A+(\alpha\vee\beta)$.

d. The proof consists of two parts:

(I) Proof that (1) and (2) imply (3): Suppose that (1) and (2) are satisfied. Let $\alpha\rightarrow\beta \in A+\beta$ and $\beta\rightarrow\alpha \in A+\alpha$. Since *extensionality* holds, it follows by Part *c* of the present exercise from $\alpha\rightarrow\beta \in A+\beta$ that $A+\beta = A+(\alpha\vee\beta)$.

Similarly, it follows from $\beta \rightarrow \alpha \in A+\alpha$ that $A+\alpha = A+(\alpha \vee \beta)$. We can conclude that $A+\alpha = A+\beta$.

(II) Proof that (3) implies (1) and (2): Suppose that (3) is satisfied. Let $\beta \in A+(\alpha\&\beta)$. In order to show that (1) and (2) are satisfied, we need to show that $A+(\alpha\&\beta) = A+\alpha$.

Since $\alpha \rightarrow (\alpha\&\beta)$ is a logical consequence of β, it follows by *closure* from $\beta \in A+(\alpha\&\beta)$, that $\alpha \rightarrow (\alpha\&\beta) \in A+(\alpha\&\beta)$. Furthermore, since $\vdash (\alpha\&\beta) \rightarrow \alpha$ it follows by *closure* that $(\alpha\&\beta) \rightarrow \alpha \in A+\alpha$. We can now apply (3) to $\alpha \rightarrow (\alpha\&\beta) \in A+(\alpha\&\beta)$ and $(\alpha\&\beta) \rightarrow \alpha \in A+\alpha$, and obtain $A+(\alpha\&\beta) = A+\alpha$, as desired.

76. a. $A \sim (p\&q) = \{p \vee q\}$ **b.** $A \sim p = \{q, p \vee q\}$ **c.** $A \sim q = \{p, p \vee q\}$
d. $A \sim (p \vee q) = \varnothing$ **e.** $A \sim (p \rightarrow q) = \{p, p \vee q\}$

77. a. Success is violated.
b. Inclusion is violated.
c. Relevance is violated.

78. Case 1, $\vdash \beta$: Then $A \sim_\gamma \beta = A$, and since $\beta \in A$ we are done.
Case 2, $\nvdash \beta$: Let $X \in \gamma(A \perp \beta)$. Then $X \in A \perp \beta$, and X is A-closed (Observation 1.36), i.e., $A \cap \mathrm{Cn}(X) \subseteq X$. It follows from $\alpha \in \mathrm{Cn}(\varnothing)$ that $\alpha \in \mathrm{Cn}(X)$, and we have assumed that $\alpha \in A$. We therefore have $\alpha \in A \cap \mathrm{Cn}(X) \subseteq X$. Since this holds for all $X \in \gamma(A \perp \beta)$, we have $\alpha \in \bigcap\gamma(A \perp \beta)$, i.e., $\alpha \in A \sim_\gamma \beta$.

79. Let $\alpha \vee \beta \in A \sim_\gamma \alpha$ and $Z \in \gamma(A \perp \alpha)$. It follows from $\alpha \vee \beta \in A \sim_\gamma \alpha = \bigcap\gamma(A \perp \alpha)$ that $\alpha \vee \beta \in Z$. Suppose that $\beta \notin Z$. Since $\beta \in A$ and $Z \in A \perp \alpha$ it then follows that $Z \cup \{\beta\} \vdash \alpha$, i.e. $Z \vdash \beta \rightarrow \alpha$. It follows from this and $\alpha \vee \beta \in Z$ that $Z \vdash \alpha$, contrary to $Z \in A \perp \alpha$. We can conclude from this contradiction that $\beta \in Z$. Since this holds for all $Z \in \gamma(A \perp \alpha)$, we can conclude that $\beta \in \bigcap\gamma(A \perp \alpha) = A \sim_\gamma \alpha$.

80. Since full meet contraction satisfies recovery, we have $A \subseteq \mathrm{Cn}((A \sim \alpha) \cup \{\alpha\})$. It also follows from $A \sim \alpha \subseteq A+\alpha$ that $\mathrm{Cn}((A \sim \alpha) \cup \{\alpha\}) \subseteq \mathrm{Cn}((A+\alpha) \cup \{\alpha\})$. It follows directly that $A \subseteq \mathrm{Cn}((A+\alpha) \cup \{\alpha\})$.

81. $(A \sim \alpha) \cap (A \sim \neg\alpha)$
$= (A \cap \mathrm{Cn}(\{\neg\alpha\})) \cap (A \cap \mathrm{Cn}(\{\alpha\}))$ (Observation 2.12.)
$= A \cap \mathrm{Cn}(\{\neg\alpha\}) \cap \mathrm{Cn}(\{\alpha\})$
$= A \cap \mathrm{Cn}(\{\alpha \vee \neg\alpha\})$ (Observation 1.17.)
$= A \cap \mathrm{Cn}(\varnothing)$
$= \mathrm{Cn}(\varnothing)$

82. a. We can use Observation 2.12 to obtain: $A\sim\alpha = A \cap \mathrm{Cn}(\{\neg\alpha\}) = \mathrm{Cn}(\{\alpha\}) \cap \mathrm{Cn}(\{\neg\alpha\}) = \mathrm{Cn}(\{\alpha\vee\neg\alpha\}) = \mathrm{Cn}(\varnothing)$. (Cf. Observation 1.17 and Exercise 2 for the last two steps.)
b. $A\sim\beta = A \cap \mathrm{Cn}(\{\neg\beta\}) = \mathrm{Cn}(\{\alpha\}) \cap \mathrm{Cn}(\{\neg\beta\}) = \mathrm{Cn}(\{\alpha\vee\neg\beta\}) = \mathrm{Cn}(\{\beta\rightarrow\alpha\})$. (Cf. Exercise 3.)

83. If α is logically true, then $A+\alpha = A$, and we are done. For the principal case, when α is not logically true, let $\beta \in A$ and $\delta \in A$. We are going to prove the converse form of the postulate, i.e., we are going to show that if $\beta \notin A+\alpha$ and $\delta \notin A+\alpha$, then $\beta\vee\delta \notin A+\alpha$.

Since + is maxichoice, $A+\alpha \in A\bot\alpha$, and it follows from $\beta \in A$ and $\beta \notin A+\alpha$ that $\alpha \in \mathrm{Cn}((A+\alpha)\cup\{\beta\})$. By the deduction property of Cn, $\beta\rightarrow\alpha \in \mathrm{Cn}(A+\alpha)$. In the same way it follows from $\delta \in A$ and $\delta \notin A+\alpha$ that $\delta\rightarrow\alpha \in \mathrm{Cn}(A+\alpha)$. Since $\beta\rightarrow\alpha$ and $\delta\rightarrow\alpha$ together imply $\beta\vee\delta\rightarrow\alpha$, we have $\beta\vee\delta\rightarrow\alpha \in \mathrm{Cn}(A+\alpha)$.

Since maxichoice contraction satisfies the success postulate, we have $\alpha \notin \mathrm{Cn}(A+\alpha)$. From $\beta\vee\delta\rightarrow\alpha \in \mathrm{Cn}(A+\alpha)$ and $\alpha \notin \mathrm{Cn}(A+\alpha)$ we can conclude that $\beta\vee\delta \notin A+\alpha$.

84. a. *Closure*: Since both $A\sim_\gamma\alpha$ and $A\sim_\gamma(\alpha\rightarrow f(\alpha))$ are logically closed, so is $A\sim_\gamma\alpha \cap A\sim_\gamma(\alpha\rightarrow f(\alpha))$.
Inclusion: It follows from $A\sim_\gamma\alpha \subseteq A$ that $A\sim_\gamma\alpha \cap A\sim_\gamma(\alpha\rightarrow f(\alpha)) \subseteq A$.
Vacuity: If $\alpha \notin \mathrm{Cn}(A)$, then if follows from clause (II) of the definition that $A+\alpha = A\sim_\gamma\alpha$. Since vacuity holds for partial meet contraction, we have $A\sim_\gamma\alpha = A$.
Success: Let $\alpha \notin \mathrm{Cn}(\varnothing)$. Since success holds for partial meet contraction, we have $\alpha \notin A\sim_\gamma\alpha$, and since $A+\alpha \subseteq A\sim_\gamma\alpha$ we can conclude that $\alpha \notin A+\alpha$.
Extensionality: From extensionality for partial meet contraction and clause (2) of the definition of f.
Failure: Let $\alpha \in \mathrm{Cn}(\varnothing)$. Then it follows from clause (II) of the definition that $A+\alpha = A\sim_\gamma\alpha$. Since partial meet contraction satisfies *failure*, we also have $A\sim_\gamma\alpha = A$, and it follows that $A+\alpha = A$.
b. Let $\alpha \in A\setminus\mathrm{Cn}(\varnothing)$ and $f(\alpha) \notin \mathrm{Cn}(\{\alpha\})$. In order to prove that $A \neq \mathrm{Cn}((A+\alpha)\cup\{\alpha\})$, suppose to the contrary that $A = \mathrm{Cn}((A+\alpha)\cup\{\alpha\})$, i.e., $A = \mathrm{Cn}((A\sim_\gamma\alpha \cap A\sim_\gamma(\alpha\rightarrow f(\alpha)))\cup\{\alpha\})$. Then $A \subseteq \mathrm{Cn}(A\sim_\gamma(\alpha\rightarrow f(\alpha))\cup\{\alpha\})$. Since $f(\alpha) \in A$, it follows that $f(\alpha) \in \mathrm{Cn}(A\sim_\gamma(\alpha\rightarrow f(\alpha))\cup\{\alpha\})$, and hence by deduction $\alpha\rightarrow f(\alpha) \in \mathrm{Cn}(A\sim_\gamma(\alpha\rightarrow f(\alpha)))$ from which it follows that $\alpha\rightarrow f(\alpha) \in \mathrm{Cn}(\varnothing)$, contrary to $f(\alpha) \notin \mathrm{Cn}(\{\alpha\})$.

85. Let $\beta \in A$. Due to the closure of A under implication, $(\alpha_1\rightarrow(\alpha_2\rightarrow\ldots(\alpha_n\rightarrow\beta))) \in A$. (Note that $(\alpha_1\rightarrow(\alpha_2\rightarrow\ldots(\alpha_n\rightarrow\beta)))$ is equivalent to $(\alpha_1\&\ldots\alpha_n)\rightarrow\beta$.)

Suppose that $(\alpha_1 \to (\alpha_2 \to ... (\alpha_n \to \beta))) \notin \cap\gamma(A\bot(\alpha_1 \& ... \& \alpha_n))$. Then there is some $X \in A\bot(\alpha_1 \& ... \& \alpha_n)$ such that $(\alpha_1 \to (\alpha_2 \to ... (\alpha_n \to \beta))) \notin X$. From this and $(\alpha_1 \to (\alpha_2 \to ... (\alpha_n \to \beta))) \in A$ follows $X \cup \{(\alpha_1 \to (\alpha_2 \to ... (\alpha_n \to \beta)))\} \vdash \alpha_1 \& ... \& \alpha_n$. Using the deduction property of Cn, we can obtain $(\alpha_1 \to (\alpha_2 \to ... (\alpha_n \to \beta))) \to (\alpha_1 \& ... \& \alpha_n) \in \text{Cn}(X)$, that is, equivalently, $(\alpha_1 \& ... \& \alpha_n \to \beta) \to (\alpha_1 \& ... \& \alpha_n) \in \text{Cn}(X)$, equivalently $\alpha_1 \& ... \& \alpha_n \in \text{Cn}(X)$. This contradicts $X \in A\bot(\alpha_1 \& ... \& \alpha_n)$, and we may conclude from this contradiction that $(\alpha_1 \to (\alpha_2 \to ... (\alpha_n \to \beta))) \in \cap\gamma(A\bot(\alpha_1 \& ... \& \alpha_n))$. From this the desired result follows directly.

86. Let $A\bot\alpha \neq \varnothing$. It follows from the definition of a selection function that $\gamma(A\bot\alpha)$ is a non-empty subset of $A\bot\alpha$. From this it follows that $\{X \in A\bot\alpha \mid A{\sim_\gamma}\alpha \subseteq X\}$ is non-empty. Since all of its elements contain $A{\sim_\gamma}\alpha$, we can conclude that $A{\sim_\gamma}\alpha \subseteq \cap\{X \in A\bot\alpha \mid A{\sim_\gamma}\alpha \subseteq X\}$.

For the other direction, i.e., $\cap\{X \in A\bot\alpha \mid A{\sim_\gamma}\alpha \subseteq X\} \subseteq A{\sim_\gamma}\alpha$, let $\beta \notin A{\sim_\gamma}\alpha$. We are going to show that $\beta \notin \cap\{X \in A\bot\alpha \mid A{\sim_\gamma}\alpha \subseteq X\}$.

It follows from $\beta \notin A{\sim_\gamma}\alpha$ that there is some $Y \in \gamma(A\bot\alpha)$ such that $\beta \notin Y$. Clearly, $A{\sim_\gamma}\alpha \subseteq Y$, so that $Y \in \{X \in A\bot\alpha \mid A{\sim_\gamma}\alpha \subseteq X\}$. It follows from this and $\beta \notin Y$ that $\beta \notin \cap\{X \in A\bot\alpha \mid A{\sim_\gamma}\alpha \subseteq X\}$, which is what we needed to complete the proof.

87. *Construction-to-postulates*: This follows from Theorem 2.7 and Exercise 83.

Postulates-to-construction: Let A be logically closed, and let $\div$ be an operator for A that satisfies *closure*, *inclusion*, *vacuity*, *success*, *extensionality*, *recovery*, and *primeness*. It follows from Theorem 2.7 that $\div$ is a partial meet contraction, i.e., there is a selection function γ for A such that $\div$ and $\sim_\gamma$ coincide ($A\div\alpha = A{\sim_\gamma}\alpha$ for all α). We need to show that $\sim_\gamma$ is a maxichoice operator, i.e., that for all α, if $\beta \in A \setminus (A{\sim_\gamma}\alpha)$, then $\alpha \in \text{Cn}((A{\sim_\gamma}\alpha) \cup \{\beta\})$. By *closure* and the deduction property of Cn, this is equivalent to showing that if $\beta \in A \setminus (A{\sim_\gamma}\alpha)$, then $\beta \to \alpha \in A{\sim_\gamma}\alpha$.

Let $\beta \in A \setminus (A{\sim_\gamma}\alpha)$. Since $\beta \vee (\beta \to \alpha) \in \text{Cn}(\varnothing)$, it follows from *closure* that $\beta \vee (\beta \to \alpha) \in A{\sim_\gamma}\alpha$. We have $\beta \in A$, and we can easily obtain $\alpha \in A$. (Since $\beta \in A \setminus (A{\sim_\gamma}\alpha)$, we have $A \neq A{\sim_\gamma}\alpha$ and we can use *vacuity* to obtain $\alpha \in A$.) It follows from *closure* that $\beta \to \alpha \in A$.Therefore, *primeness* can be applied, and it yields that either $\beta \in A{\sim_\gamma}\alpha$ or $\beta \to \alpha \in A{\sim_\gamma}\alpha$. Since the former is precluded by our initial condition for β, it follows that $\beta \to \alpha \in A{\sim_\gamma}\alpha$. This is what was required to finish the proof.

88. a. Let γ be defined as follows:

(i) If $A\bot\alpha \neq \varnothing$, then $\gamma(A\bot\alpha) = \{X \in A\bot\alpha \mid A\div\alpha \subseteq X\}$

(ii) If $A\bot\alpha = \varnothing$, then $\gamma(A\bot\alpha) = \{A\}$

We need to show (1) that γ is a function, (2) that γ is a selection function (from which follows that $\sim_\gamma$ is an operator of partial meet contraction), and (3) that $A{\div}\alpha \subseteq A{\sim_\gamma}\alpha$ for all α.

Part 1: Let $A\perp\alpha = A\perp\beta$. It follows from *uniformity* and Observation 1.39 that $A{\div}\alpha = A{\div}\beta$, and thus, according to our definition of γ, $\gamma(A\perp\alpha) = \gamma(A\perp\beta)$.

Part 2: We need to show that if $A\perp\alpha$ is non-empty, then so is $\gamma(A\perp\alpha)$. Suppose that $A\perp\alpha \neq \varnothing$. Then $\nvdash\alpha$, and by *success* $\alpha \notin \mathrm{Cn}(A{\div}\alpha)$. By *inclusion*, $A{\div}\alpha \subseteq A$. It follows from the upper bound property that there is some set X such that $A{\div}\alpha \subseteq X \in A\perp\alpha$. By the construction of γ, $X \in \gamma(A\perp\alpha)$, so that $\gamma(A\perp\alpha) \neq \varnothing$.

Part 3: This follows directly from the definition.

b. We can use Observation 2.4 to conclude that *uniformity* holds. The rest follows as in Part *a*.

89. *Construction-to-postulates*: Let $\sim_\gamma$ be an operation of partial meet package contraction for A.

P-success: Suppose that $B\cap\mathrm{Cn}(\varnothing) = \varnothing$. Then $A\perp B \neq \varnothing$, and it follows from Definition 2.61 that $\gamma(A\perp B)$ is a non-empty subset of $A\perp B$. Let $X \in \gamma(A\perp B)$. Then it follows from $X \in A\perp B$ that $B\cap\mathrm{Cn}(X) = \varnothing$. Furthermore, it follows from $X \in \gamma(A\perp B)$ that $\cap\gamma(A\perp B) \subseteq X$, so that $\mathrm{Cn}(\cap\gamma(A\perp B)) \subseteq \mathrm{Cn}(X)$. We can conclude that $B\cap\mathrm{Cn}(\cap\gamma(A\perp B)) = \varnothing$.

P-inclusion: If $A\perp B$ is empty, then by Definition 2.61 $A{\sim_\gamma}B = A$, and we are done. If $A\perp B$ is non-empty, then by the same definition $\gamma(A\perp B)$ is a subset of $A\perp B$. It follows that every element of $\gamma(A\perp B)$ is a subset of A, and then so is $\cap\gamma(A\perp B)$.

P-relevance: Let $\beta \in A$ and $\beta \notin A{\sim_\gamma}B$. It follows from Definition 2.61 that there is some A' such that $\beta \notin A' \in \gamma(A\perp B)$. Clearly, $A{\sim_\gamma}B \subseteq A' \subseteq A$. It follows from $A' \in A\perp B$ that $B\cap\mathrm{Cn}(A') = \varnothing$. It also follows from $\beta \in A$ and $\beta \notin X \in A\perp B$ that $B\cap\mathrm{Cn}(A'\cup\{\beta\}) \neq \varnothing$.

P-uniformity: Let B_1 and B_2 be two sets such that any subset of A implies B_1 if and only if it implies B_2. It follows from Observation 1.39 that $A\perp B_1 = A\perp B_2$. From this it follows directly by Definition 2.61 that $A{\div}B_1 = A{\div}B_2$.

Postulates-to-construction: Let $\div$ be an operation for A that satisfies *P-success*, *P-inclusion*, *P-relevance*, and *P-uniformity*. Let γ be such that:

(i) If $A\perp B \neq \varnothing$, then $\gamma(A\perp B) = \{X \in A\perp B \mid A{\div}B \subseteq X\}$

(ii) If $A\perp B = \varnothing$, then $\gamma(A\perp B) = \{A\}$

We need to show (1) that γ is a (well-defined) function, (2) that γ is a package selection function, and (3) that for all B, $\cap\gamma(A\perp B) = A{\div}B$.

Part 1: In order for γ to be a function, it must be the case that for all B_1 and B_2, if $A\perp B_1 = A\perp B_2$, then $\gamma(A\perp B_1) = \gamma(A\perp B_2)$. Suppose that $A\perp B_1 = A\perp B_2$. It then follows from Observation 1.39 that any subset of A implies some element of B_1 if and only if it implies some element of B_2. By *P-uniformity*, $A+B_1 = A+B_2$. It follows from the definition of γ that $\gamma(A\perp B_1) = \gamma(A\perp B_2)$.

Part 2: In order to prove that γ is a package selection function, it is sufficient to show that if $A\perp B$ is non-empty, then so is $\gamma(A\perp B)$. Suppose that $A\perp B$ is non-empty. Then $B\cap\text{Cn}(\varnothing) = \varnothing$, and it follows from *P-success* that $B\cap\text{Cn}(A+B) = \varnothing$. It follows from *P-inclusion* that $A+B \subseteq A$. By the upper bound property, there is some D such that $A+B \subseteq D \in A\perp B$. By the construction of γ, $D \in \gamma(A\perp\alpha)$, which proves that $\gamma(A\perp\alpha)$ is non-empty.

Part 3: There are two cases, according to whether or not $B\cap\text{Cn}(\varnothing)$ is empty.

First case, $B\cap\text{Cn}(\varnothing) \neq \varnothing$: It follows that $A\perp B = \varnothing$. Our definition of γ yields $\gamma(A\perp B) = \{A\}$, and thus $\cap\gamma(A\perp B) = A$. It remains to be shown that $A+B = A$.

By *P-inclusion*, $A+B \subseteq A$. In order to show that $A \subseteq A+B$, suppose to the contrary that this is not the case. Then there is some ε such that $\varepsilon \in A$ and $\varepsilon \notin A+B$. It follows from *P-relevance* that there is some set A' such that $A+B \subseteq A' \subseteq A$ and $B\cap\text{Cn}(A') = \varnothing$ but $B\cap\text{Cn}(A'\cup\{\varepsilon\}) \neq \varnothing$. This, however, is impossible. Since $B\cap\text{Cn}(\varnothing) \neq \varnothing$, it cannot hold that $B\cap\text{Cn}(A') = \varnothing$. From this contradiction we may conclude that $A \subseteq A+B$, and thus $A+B = A$.

Second case, $B\cap\text{Cn}(\varnothing) = \varnothing$: In this case, $A\perp B$ is non-empty, and we have shown in Part 2 of the present proof that $\gamma(A\perp B)$ is also non-empty. It follows from our definition of γ that $A+B$ is a a subset of every element of $\gamma(A\perp B)$, from which we may conclude that $A+B \subseteq \cap\gamma(A\perp B)$.

In order to show that $\cap\gamma(A\perp B) \subseteq A+B$, let $\varepsilon \notin A+B$. We are going to show that $\varepsilon \notin \cap\gamma(A\perp B)$. This is obvious if $\varepsilon \notin A$. In the remaining case, when $\varepsilon \in A$, we have $\varepsilon \in A$ and $\varepsilon \notin A+B$. It follows from *P-relevance* that there is some set A' such that $A+B \subseteq A' \subseteq A$, $B\cap\text{Cn}(A') = \varnothing$ and $B\cap\text{Cn}(A'\cup\{\varepsilon\}) \neq \varnothing$. It follows by the upper bound property from $A' \subseteq A$ and $B\cap\text{Cn}(A') = \varnothing$ that there is some set D such that $A' \subseteq D \in A\perp B$. Clearly, $\varepsilon \notin D$. It follows from $A+B \subseteq A' \subseteq D$, by our definition of γ, that $D \in \gamma(A\perp B)$. From this and $\varepsilon \notin D$ we can conclude that $\varepsilon \notin \cap\gamma(A\perp B)$. This concludes the proof.

90. a. Yes, since $A\perp\{\alpha,\alpha\} = A\perp\{\alpha\}$.
b. Yes, since if $\beta \notin \text{Cn}(A)$, then $A\perp\{\alpha,\beta\} = A\perp\{\alpha\}$.
c. Yes. Observation 1.40 yields $A\perp\{\alpha\} = A\perp\{\alpha\&\beta, \alpha\}$
d. Yes. Observation 1.40 yields $A\perp\{\alpha,\beta\} = A\perp\{\alpha\&\beta, \alpha, \beta\}$
e. No. It does not hold in general that $A\perp\{\alpha\&\beta\} = A\perp\{\alpha, \beta\}$. For a counter-example, let $A = \{p,q,p\leftrightarrow q\}$. Then $A\perp\{p\&q\} = \{\{p\},\{q\},\{p\leftrightarrow q\}\}$ and $A\perp\{p,q\} = \{\{p\leftrightarrow q\}\}$. Let $\gamma(A\perp\{p\&q\}) = \{\{p\}\}$ and $\gamma(A\perp\{p,q\}) = \{\{p\leftrightarrow q\}\}$. We then have $A+\{p\&q\} = \{p\}$ and $A+\{p,q\} = \{p\leftrightarrow q\}$.

91. Let Γ be the covering function that generates the subremainder contraction $\div$ for a logically closed set A.

P-closure: $A \div B = \cap\Gamma(B)$ is the intersection of a set of remainders of A. Since A is logically closed set, so are all its remainders (Observation 1.48). The intersection of a set of logically closed sets is logically closed (Observation 1.25).

P-inclusion: Every element of $\Gamma(B)$ is a subset of A, and consequently so is $\cap\Gamma(B)$.

P-vacuity: Let $B \cap Cn(A) = \emptyset$. It follows that $A \perp \beta = \{A\}$ for every $\beta \in B$, and thus $A \Delta B = \{A\}$, $\Gamma(B) = \{A\}$ and $\cap\Gamma(B) = A$.

P-success: Let $B \cap Cn(\emptyset) = \emptyset$. It follows from Definition 2.64 that $\Gamma(B)$ is a subset of $A \Delta B$ such that $\Gamma(B) \cap (A \perp \beta) \neq \emptyset$ for all $\beta \in B$.

Let $\beta \in B$. There is then some $X \in A \perp \beta$ such that $X \in \Gamma(B)$ and consequently $\cap\Gamma(B) \subseteq X$. It follows from $\beta \notin X$ that $\beta \notin \cap\Gamma(B)$.

P-failure: Let $B \cap Cn(\emptyset) \neq \emptyset$. It follows from Definition 2.64 that $\Gamma(B) = \{A\}$, and consequently $\cap\Gamma(B) = A$.

92. a. *(1) implies (2)*: Let X be such that $D \subseteq X \subseteq A$, $B \cap Cn(X) = \emptyset$, and $B \cap Cn(X \cup \{\beta\}) \neq \emptyset$. It follows from the upper bound property that there is some X' such that $X \subseteq X' \in A \perp B$. To see that (2) is satisfied, it is sufficient to note that $D \subseteq X' \in A \perp B$ and that $\beta \notin X'$. (The latter can be concluded from $X \subseteq X'$, $B \cap Cn(X') = \emptyset$, and $B \cap Cn(X \cup \{\beta\}) \neq \emptyset$.)

(2) implies (1): Let X be such that $D \subseteq X \in A \perp B$ and $\beta \notin X$. Then we directly have $D \subseteq X \subseteq A$ and $B \cap Cn(X) = \emptyset$. Since $\beta \in A$, but $\beta \notin X \in A \perp B$, it follows from the maximality of remainders that $B \cap Cn(X \cup \{\beta\}) \neq \emptyset$.

b. *P-relevance* has been defined as follows:

(1) If $\beta \in A$ and $\beta \notin A \div B$, then there is a set A' such that $A \div B \subseteq A' \subseteq A$ and that $B \cap Cn(A') = \emptyset$ but $B \cap Cn(A' \cup \{\beta\}) \neq \emptyset$.

By Part *a*, this is equivalent to:

(2) If $\beta \in A$ and $\beta \notin A \div B$, then there is some X such that $A \div B \subseteq X \in A \perp B$ and $\beta \notin X$.

This is equivalent to:

(3) If $\beta \in A$ and $\beta \notin A \div B$, then $\{X \mid A \div B \subseteq X \in A \perp B\}$ is non-empty and $\beta \notin \cap\{X \mid A \div B \subseteq X \in A \perp B\}$

Since *P-success* is satisfied and B contains no logically true sentence, $\{X \mid A \div B \subseteq X \in A \perp B\}$ is non-empty, and (3) is equivalent to:

(4) If $\beta \in A$ and $\beta \notin A \div B$, then $\beta \notin \cap\{X \mid A \div B \subseteq X \in A \perp B\}$

If $\beta \notin A$, then β is not included in any element of $A \perp B$. Therefore, we can simplify (4) as follows:

(5) If $\beta \notin A \div B$, then $\beta \notin \cap\{X \mid A \div B \subseteq X \in A \perp B\}$

(6) $\cap\{X \mid A \div B \subseteq X \in A \perp B\} \subseteq A \div B$

Finally, since $\{X \mid A \div B \subseteq X \in A \perp B\}$ is non-empty, (6) is equivalent to:

(7) $A{+}B = \cap\{X \mid A{+}B \subseteq X \in A\bot B\}$.

93. a. *Construction-to-postulates*: Let $\sim_\gamma$ be an operation of partial meet choice contraction for A.

C-success: For this part of the proof, let $B \not\subseteq \mathrm{Cn}(\varnothing)$. Then $A\angle B$ is non-empty, so that that $\gamma(A\angle B)$ is a non-empty subset of $A\angle B$. Let $X \in \gamma(A\angle B)$. Then it follows from $X \in A\angle B$ that $B \not\subseteq \mathrm{Cn}(X)$. Furthermore, it follows from $X \in \gamma(A\angle B)$ that $\cap\gamma(A\angle B) \subseteq X$, so that $\mathrm{Cn}(\cap\gamma(A\angle B)) \subseteq \mathrm{Cn}(X)$. We can conclude that $B \not\subseteq \mathrm{Cn}(\cap\gamma(A\angle B))$.

C-inclusion: If $A\angle B$ is empty, then $A\sim_\gamma B = A$, and we are done. If $A\angle B$ is non-empty, then $\gamma(A\angle B)$ is a subset of $A\angle B$. It follows that every element of $\gamma(A\angle B)$ is a subset of A, and then so is $\cap\gamma(A\angle B)$.

C-relevance: Let $\beta \in A$ and $\beta \notin A\sim_\gamma B$. It follows that there is some A' such that $\beta \notin A' \in \gamma(A\angle B)$. Clearly, $A\sim_\gamma B \subseteq A' \subseteq A$. It follows from $A' \in A\angle B$ that $B \not\subseteq \mathrm{Cn}(A') = \varnothing$. It also follows from $\beta \in A$ and $\beta \notin X \in A\angle B$ that $B \subseteq \mathrm{Cn}(A' \cup \{\beta\})$.

C-uniformity: Let B_1 and B_2 be such that $B_1 \subseteq \mathrm{Cn}(X)$ iff $B_2 \subseteq \mathrm{Cn}(X)$ for all $X \subseteq A$. We are first going to show that $A\angle B_1 = A\angle B_2$.

Let $X \in A\angle B_1$. It follows directly that (1) $X \subseteq A$, (2) $B_2 \not\subseteq \mathrm{Cn}(X)$, and (3) if $X \subset Y \subseteq A$, then $B_2 \subseteq \mathrm{Cn}(Y)$. Thus, $X \in A\angle B_2$. It follows in exactly the same way that if $X \in A\angle B_2$, then $X \in A\angle B_1$. Thus, $A\angle B_1 = A\angle B_2$.

It follows from $A\angle B_1 = A\angle B_2$ that $\cap\gamma(A\angle B_1) = \cap\gamma(A\angle B_2)$.

Postulates-to-construction: Let $+$ be an operation for A that satisfies *C-success*, *C-inclusion*, *C-relevance*, and *C-uniformity*. Let γ be such that:

(i) If $A\angle B \neq \varnothing$, then $\gamma(A\angle B) = \{X \in A\angle B \mid A{+}B \subseteq X\}$

(ii) If $A\angle B = \varnothing$, then $\gamma(A\angle B) = \{A\}$

We need to show (1) that γ is a (well-defined) function, (2) that γ is a choice selection function, and (3) that for all B, $\cap\gamma(A\angle B) = A{+}B$.

Part 1: In order for γ to be a function, it must be the case that for all B_1 and B_2, if $A\angle B_1 = A\angle B_2$, then $\gamma(A\angle B_1) = \gamma(A\angle B_2)$. Let $A\angle B_1 = A\angle B_2$. It follows that $B_1 \subseteq \mathrm{Cn}(X)$ iff $B_2 \subseteq \mathrm{Cn}(X)$ for all $X \subseteq A$. By *C-uniformity*, $A{+}B_1 = A{+}B_2$. From this it follows by the definition of γ that $\gamma(A\angle B_1) = \gamma(A\angle B_2)$.

Part 2: For γ to be a selection function, it must be the case that if $A\angle B \neq \varnothing$, then $\gamma(A\angle B) \neq \varnothing$. Let $A\angle B \neq \varnothing$. Then $B \not\subseteq \mathrm{Cn}(\varnothing)$, and it follows by *C-success* that $B \not\subseteq \mathrm{Cn}(A{+}B)$. By *C-inclusion*, $A{+}B \subseteq A$. It follows by the upper bound property (or rather, by its corresponding version for $\angle$) that there is some Z such that $A{+}B \subseteq Z \in A\angle B$. By our definition of γ, $Z \in \gamma(A\angle B)$.

Part 3: There are two cases, according to whether or not $B \subseteq \mathrm{Cn}(\varnothing)$.

First case, $B \subseteq \mathrm{Cn}(\varnothing)$: It follows that $A\angle B = \varnothing$. Our definition of γ yields $\gamma(A\angle B) = \{A\}$, and thus $\cap\gamma(A\angle B) = A$. It remains to be shown that $A{+}B = A$.

By *C-inclusion*, $A{+}B \subseteq A$. In order to show that $A \subseteq A{+}B$, suppose to the contrary that this is not the case. Then there is some ε such that $\varepsilon \in A$ and $\varepsilon \notin A{+}B$. It follows by *C-relevance* that there is some set A' such that $A{+}B \subseteq A' \subseteq A$ and $B \not\subseteq \mathrm{Cn}(A')$ and $B \subseteq \mathrm{Cn}(A'\cup\{\varepsilon\}) \neq \emptyset$. This, however, is impossible. Since $B \subseteq \mathrm{Cn}(\emptyset)$, it cannot hold that $B \not\subseteq \mathrm{Cn}(A')$. From this contradiction we may conclude that $A \subseteq A{+}B$, and thus $A{+}B = A$.

Second case, $B \not\subseteq \mathrm{Cn}(\emptyset)$: In this case, $A\angle B$ is non-empty, and we have shown in Part 2 of the present proof that $\gamma(A\angle B)$ is non-empty as well. It follows by our definition of γ that $A{+}B$ is asubset of every element of $\gamma(A\angle B)$, from which we may conclude that $A{+}B \subseteq \cap\gamma(A\angle B)$.

In order to show that $\cap\gamma(A\angle B) \subseteq A{+}B$, let $\varepsilon \notin A{+}B$. We are going to show that $\varepsilon \notin \cap\gamma(A\angle B)$. This is obvious if $\varepsilon \notin A$. In the remaining case we have $\varepsilon \in A$ and $\varepsilon \notin A{+}B$. It follows from *C-relevance* that there is some set A' such that $A{+}B \subseteq A' \subseteq A$, $B \not\subseteq \mathrm{Cn}(A')$ and $B \subseteq \mathrm{Cn}(A'\cup\{\varepsilon\})$. It follows by (the variant for $\angle$ of) the upper bound property from $A' \subseteq A$ and $B \not\subseteq \mathrm{Cn}(A') = \emptyset$ that there is some set D such that $A' \subseteq D \in A\angle B$. Clearly, $\varepsilon \notin D$. It follows from $A{+}B \subseteq A' \subseteq D$, by our definition of γ, that $D \in \gamma(A\angle B)$. From this and $\varepsilon \notin D$ we can conclude that $\varepsilon \notin \cap\gamma(A\angle B)$. This concludes the proof.

b. For any finite set B, $B \subseteq \mathrm{Cn}(A)$ if and only if $\&B \in \mathrm{Cn}(A)$. It follows from this that for all finite B, $A\angle B = A\angle(\&B) = A\perp(\&B)$. It is therefore sufficient to let $+'$ be the restriction of $+$ to remainders with singleton rejectors.

94. According to Observation 2.68, $\cap\gamma(A\perp\alpha) = \cap\hat{\gamma}(A\perp\alpha)$. We therefore have $\hat{\hat{\gamma}}(A\perp\alpha) = \{X \mid \cap\hat{\gamma}(A\perp\alpha) \subseteq X \in A\perp\alpha\} = \{X \mid \cap\gamma(A\perp\alpha) \subseteq X \in A\perp\alpha\} = \hat{\gamma}(A\perp\alpha)$.

95. It follows set-theoretically from $\gamma_1(A\perp\alpha) \subseteq \gamma_2(A\perp\alpha)$ that $\cap\gamma_2(A\perp\alpha) \subseteq \cap\gamma_1(A\perp\alpha)$. In the same way it follows from $\gamma_2(A\perp\alpha) \subseteq \hat{\gamma}_1(A\perp\alpha)$ that $\cap\hat{\gamma}_1(A\perp\alpha) \subseteq \cap\gamma_2(A\perp\alpha)$. Since $\cap\hat{\gamma}_1(A\perp\alpha) = \cap\gamma_1(A\perp\alpha)$ (Observation 2.68), we can conclude that $\cap\gamma_1(A\perp\alpha) = \cap\gamma_2(A\perp\alpha)$.

96. It follows set-theoretically from $\gamma(A\perp\alpha) \subseteq \gamma(A\perp\beta)$ that $\cap\gamma(A\perp\beta) \subseteq \cap\gamma(A\perp\alpha)$.

Let $X \in \hat{\gamma}(A\perp\alpha)$. Then $\cap\hat{\gamma}(A\perp\alpha) \subseteq X$. Since $\cap\hat{\gamma}(A\perp\alpha) = \cap\gamma(A\perp\alpha)$ (Observation 2.68), we have $\cap\gamma(A\perp\alpha) \subseteq X$. We can conclude from this and $\cap\gamma(A\perp\beta) \subseteq \cap\gamma(A\perp\alpha)$ that $\cap\gamma(A\perp\beta) \subseteq X$. It follows from $\cap\gamma(A\perp\beta) \subseteq X \in A\perp\alpha$, by Observation 2.69, that $X \in \hat{\gamma}(A\perp\beta)$.

97. a. It follows set-theoretically from $\gamma(A\perp\beta) \subseteq \gamma(A\perp\alpha)$ that $\cap\gamma(A\perp\alpha) \subseteq \cap\gamma(A\perp\beta)$, i.e., $A{\sim_\gamma}\alpha \subseteq A{\sim_\gamma}\beta$. For the other direction, let $A{\sim_\gamma}\alpha \subseteq A{\sim_\gamma}\beta$ and let $X \in \gamma(A\perp\beta)$. Then $\cap\gamma(A\perp\beta) \subseteq X$, i.e., $A{\sim_\gamma}\beta \subseteq X$. Since $A{\sim_\gamma}\alpha \subseteq A{\sim_\gamma}\beta$ it follows that $A{\sim}_\gamma\alpha \subseteq X \in A\perp\beta$. It follows from Part 2 of Observation 2.69 that $X \in \gamma(A\perp\alpha)$.

b. If $(A{\sim}_\gamma\alpha)\cup(A{\sim}_\gamma\beta) \nvdash \alpha$, then there is by the upper bound property some X such that $(A{\sim}_\gamma\alpha)\cup(A{\sim}_\gamma\beta) \subseteq X \in A\perp\alpha$. By applying Observation 2.69, to $A{\sim}_\gamma\alpha \subseteq X \in A\perp\alpha$, we obtain $X \in \gamma(A\perp\alpha)$, and by applying it to $A{\sim}_\gamma\beta \subseteq X \in A\perp\alpha$, we obtain $X \in \gamma(A\perp\beta)$. We have established that $X \in \gamma(A\perp\alpha) \cap \gamma(A\perp\beta)$, and thus $\gamma(A\perp\alpha) \cap \gamma(A\perp\beta) \neq \varnothing$.

98. *I implies II*: Since $\div$ is an operator of partial meet contraction, it is based on some selection function γ, and by Observation 2.68 it is also based on $\hat{\gamma}$, the completion of γ.

Suppose that (I) holds. In order to show that (II) holds for $\hat{\gamma}$, suppose that $\alpha, \beta \in A\backslash Cn(\varnothing)$, $\beta \notin \cap\hat{\gamma}(A\perp\alpha\&\beta)$, and $X \in \hat{\gamma}(A\perp\alpha)$.

It follows from $X \in \hat{\gamma}(A\perp\alpha)$ that $\cap\hat{\gamma}(A\perp\alpha) \subseteq X$. From (I) we have $A\div(\alpha\&\beta) \subseteq A\div\alpha$, i.e., $\cap\hat{\gamma}(A\perp\alpha\&\beta) \subseteq \cap\hat{\gamma}(A\perp\alpha)$. Thus, $\cap\hat{\gamma}(A\perp\alpha\&\beta) \subseteq X$. It follows by Observation 1.53 from $X \in A\perp\alpha$ that $X \in A\perp(\alpha\&\beta)$. We therefore have $\cap\hat{\gamma}(A\perp\alpha\&\beta) \subseteq X \in A\perp(\alpha\&\beta)$, and it follows from the completion property that $X \in \hat{\gamma}(A\perp\alpha\&\beta)$.

II implies I: There are four limiting cases:

Case 1, $\vdash\alpha$: Then $A\div\alpha = A$, so that $A\div(\alpha\&\beta) \subseteq A\div\alpha$ holds.

Case 2, $\vdash\beta$: Then $\beta \in A\div(\alpha\&\beta)$, and (I) is vacuously satisfied.

Case 3, $\alpha \notin A$: Then $A\div\alpha = A$, so that $A\div(\alpha\&\beta) \subseteq A\div\alpha$ holds.

Case 4, $\beta \notin A$: Then (I) holds vacuously.

Case 5, $\alpha, \beta \in A\backslash Cn(\varnothing)$: Suppose that $\beta \notin A\div(\alpha\&\beta)$, i.e., $\beta \notin \cap\gamma(A\perp\alpha\&\beta)$. It follows from (II) that $\gamma(A\perp\alpha) \subseteq \gamma(A\perp(\alpha\&\beta))$, and from this that $\cap\gamma(A\perp(\alpha\&\beta)) \subseteq \cap\gamma(A\perp\alpha)$, i.e., $A\div(\alpha\&\beta) \subseteq A\div\alpha$.

99. a. It follows from Observation 1.55 that $X, Y \in A\perp(\alpha\&\beta)$. Let $Z \in \gamma(A\perp(\alpha\&\beta))$. Then $X\sqsubseteq Z$ and $Y\sqsubseteq Z$.

b. Let $X \in \gamma(A\perp(\alpha\&\beta))\cap(A\perp\alpha)$. In order to show that $X \in \gamma(A\perp\alpha)$ we need to show that if $Y \in A\perp\alpha$, then $Y\sqsubseteq X$.

Let $Y \in A\perp\alpha$. It follows from Observation 1.55 that $Y \in A\perp(\alpha\&\beta)$. We can conclude from $X \in \gamma(A\perp(\alpha\&\beta))$ that $Y\sqsubseteq X$.

100. a. Let $A\perp\alpha \subseteq A\perp\beta$ and $A{\sim}_\gamma\beta \nvdash \alpha$. Since ${\sim}_\gamma$ is maxichoice, $A{\sim}_\gamma\beta \in \gamma(A\perp\beta)$, and we can conclude from $A{\sim}_\gamma\beta \nvdash \alpha$, by Observation 1.53 that $A{\sim}_\gamma\beta \in A\perp\alpha$.

Let $X \in A\perp\alpha$. Since $A\perp\alpha \subseteq A\perp\beta$ we then have $X \in A\perp\beta$. We can conclude from this and $A{\sim}_\gamma\beta \in \gamma(A\perp\beta)$ that $X\sqsubseteq(A{\sim}_\gamma\beta)$. Since this holds for all $X \in A\perp\beta$, we can conclude that $A{\sim}_\gamma\beta \in \gamma(A\perp\alpha)$ and, since γ is maxichoice, that $\{A{\sim}_\gamma\beta\} = \gamma(A\perp\alpha)$, so that $A{\sim}_\gamma\alpha = A{\sim}_\gamma\beta$.

b. It follows from Observation 1.54 that $\vdash \beta\rightarrow\alpha$ holds if and only if $A\bot\alpha \subseteq A\bot\beta$. Furthermore, since $A\sim_\gamma\beta$ is logically closed, $\alpha \in A\sim_\gamma\beta$ holds if and only if $A\sim_\gamma\beta \vdash \alpha$. Using these two equivalences, we can obtain the desired result directly from Part *a*.

c. Suppose to the contrary that $A\sim_\gamma(\alpha\&\beta) \neq A\sim_\gamma\alpha$ and $A\sim_\gamma(\alpha\&\beta) \neq A\sim_\gamma\beta$. It follows from Part *b* that either $\alpha \in A\sim_\gamma(\alpha\&\beta)$ or $A\sim_\gamma(\alpha\&\beta) = A\sim_\gamma\alpha$. Thus, $\alpha \in A\sim_\gamma(\alpha\&\beta)$. It follows in the same way that $\beta \in A\sim_\gamma(\alpha\&\beta)$. We can use *closure* to conclude that $\alpha\&\beta \in A\sim_\gamma(\alpha\&\beta)$. However, since both α and β are elements of $A\backslash\mathrm{Cn}(\varnothing)$, $\alpha\&\beta \notin \mathrm{Cn}(\varnothing)$, and *success* yields $\alpha\&\beta \notin A\sim_\gamma(\alpha\&\beta)$. This contradiction concludes the proof.

101. *Choice-distributivity implies property* α: Suppose that choice-distributivity is satisfied, and that $\alpha, \beta \in A\backslash\mathrm{Cn}(\varnothing)$ and $A\bot\alpha \subseteq A\bot\beta$. We are going to show that $(A\bot\alpha)\cap\gamma(A\bot\beta) \subseteq \gamma(A\bot\alpha)$.

It follows from $A\bot\alpha \subseteq A\bot\beta$, by Observation 1.54, that $\vdash \beta\rightarrow\alpha$. It follows from this that β is equivalent with $\alpha\&(\alpha\rightarrow\beta)$. It follows from choice-distributivity that $\gamma(A\bot(\alpha\&(\alpha\rightarrow\beta))) \subseteq \gamma(A\bot\alpha) \cup \gamma(A\bot(\alpha\rightarrow\beta))$, i.e., $\gamma(A\bot\beta) \subseteq \gamma(A\bot\alpha) \cup \gamma(A\bot(\alpha\rightarrow\beta))$. Intersect both sides of this last expression with $A\bot\alpha$. We obtain:

$$(A\bot\alpha)\cap(\gamma(A\bot\beta)) \subseteq (A\bot\alpha)\cap(\gamma(A\bot\alpha)\cup\gamma(A\bot(\alpha\rightarrow\beta)))$$

and consequently (by set theory)

$$(A\bot\alpha)\cap(\gamma(A\bot\beta)) \subseteq ((A\bot\alpha)\cap(\gamma(A\bot\alpha))) \cup ((A\bot\alpha)\cap\gamma(A\bot(\alpha\rightarrow\beta)))$$

This expression can be simplified. Since $\gamma(A\bot\alpha) \subseteq A\bot\alpha$, we have $(A\bot\alpha)\cap(\gamma(A\bot\alpha)) = \gamma(A\bot\alpha)$. Furthermore, since $A\bot(\alpha\rightarrow\beta) = (A\bot\beta)\backslash(A\bot\alpha)$ (Observation 1.65), $(A\bot\alpha)\cap(A\bot(\alpha\rightarrow\beta)) = \varnothing$, and consequently $(A\bot\alpha)\cap\gamma(A\bot(\alpha\rightarrow\beta)) = \varnothing$. We therefore obtain:

$$(A\bot\alpha)\cap(\gamma(A\bot\beta)) \subseteq \cap\gamma(A\bot\alpha),$$

which finishes this part of the proof.

Property α *implies choice-distributivity*: Suppose that property α is satisfied and that $\alpha, \beta \in A\backslash\mathrm{Cn}(\varnothing)$. Let $X \in \gamma(A\bot(\alpha\&\beta))$. Our task is to show that $X \in \gamma(A\bot\alpha) \cup \gamma(A\bot\beta)$.

It follows from $X \in A\bot(\alpha\&\beta)$ by Observation 1.55 that either $X \in A\bot\alpha$ or $X \in A\bot\beta$.

Case 1, $X \in A\bot\alpha$: According to Observation 1.54, $A\bot\alpha \subseteq A\bot(\alpha\&\beta)$. It follows from $A\bot\alpha \subseteq A\bot(\alpha\&\beta)$, $X \in \gamma(A\bot(\alpha\&\beta))$ and $X \in A\bot\alpha$, by property α, that $X \in \gamma(A\bot\alpha)$.

Case 2, $X \in A\bot\beta$: It follows in the same way that $X \in \gamma(A\bot\beta)$.

Thus, in both cases $X \in \gamma(A\bot\alpha) \cup \gamma(A\bot\beta)$. This finishes the proof.

102. *Part* 2: It follows from $X \sqsubset Y$ that $X \sqsubseteq Y$, and by transitivity from $X \sqsubseteq Y$ and $Y \sqsubseteq Z$ that $X \sqsubseteq Z$.

Suppose that $Z \sqsubseteq X$. Since $Y \sqsubseteq Z$ it then follows by transitivity that $Y \sqsubseteq X$, contrary to $X \sqsubset Y$. We may conclude from this contradiction that $\neg(Z \sqsubseteq X)$. Since we already have $X \sqsubseteq Z$, we may conclude that $X \sqsubset Z$.

Part 3: Let $X \sqsubset Y$ & $Y \sqsubset Z$. We then have $X \sqsubseteq Y$ & $Y \sqsubset Z$, and it follows from Part 1 of the present proof that $X \sqsubset Z$.

103. a. $X \sqsubset Y$ follows from the maximizing property. We therefore have $X \sqsubset Y \sqsubseteq Z$. It follows from the transitivity of $\sqsubseteq$ that $X \sqsubset Z$ (cf. Observation 2.75).
b. $Y \sqsubset Z$ follows from the maximizing property. We therefore have $X \sqsubseteq Y \sqsubset Z$. It follows from the transitivity of $\sqsubseteq$ that $X \sqsubset Z$ (cf. Observation 2.75).
c. There are two cases, $X \subset Y \sqsubset Z$ and $X = Y \sqsubset Z$.

If $X \subset Y \sqsubset Z$, then $X \sqsubset Y$ follows from the maximizing property, and we have $X \sqsubset Y \sqsubset Z$. It follows from the transitivity of $\sqsubseteq$ that $X \sqsubset Z$ (cf. Observation 2.75).

If $X = Y \sqsubset Z$, then $X \sqsubset Z$ follows directly from $Y \sqsubset Z$.
d. There are two cases, $X \sqsubset Y \subset Z$ and $X \sqsubset Y = Z$.

If $X \sqsubset Y \subset Z$, then $Y \sqsubset Z$ follows from the maximizing property, and we have $X \sqsubset Y \sqsubset Z$. It follows from the transitivity of $\sqsubseteq$ that $X \sqsubset Z$ (cf. Observation 2.75).

If $X \sqsubset Y = Z$, then $X \sqsubset Z$ follows directly from $X \sqsubset Y$.
e. There are two cases, $X \subset Y \sqsubseteq Z$ and $X = Y \sqsubseteq Z$.

If $X \subset Y \sqsubseteq Z$, then $X \sqsubseteq Z$ follows from Part *a*.

If $X = Y \sqsubseteq Z$, then $X \sqsubseteq Z$ follows directly from $Y \sqsubseteq Z$.
f. There are two cases, $X \sqsubseteq Y \subset Z$ and $X \sqsubseteq Y = Z$.

If $X \sqsubseteq Y \subset Z$, then $X \sqsubseteq Z$ follows from Part *b*.

If $X \sqsubseteq Y = Z$, then $X \sqsubseteq Z$ follows directly from $X \sqsubseteq Y$.

104. In order to show that $Y \in \gamma(A \perp \alpha)$ we must show that $Z \sqsubseteq Y$ for all $Z \in A \perp \alpha$. Let $Z \in A \perp \alpha$.

It follows from $X \in \gamma(A \perp \alpha)$ that $Z \sqsubseteq X$. Since $\sqsubseteq$ is transitive, we can conclude from $Z \sqsubseteq X$ and $X \sqsubseteq Y$ that $Z \sqsubseteq Y$.

105. a. Let γ be as stated in the theorem, and let $A \sim_\gamma \alpha \in A \perp \beta$ and $A \sim_\gamma \beta \in A \perp \alpha$. Since γ is maxichoice, we have $\gamma(A \perp \alpha) = \{A \sim_\gamma \alpha\}$ and $\gamma(A \perp \beta) = \{A \sim_\gamma \beta\}$. It follows from $A \sim_\gamma \beta \in A \perp \alpha$ and $\gamma(A \perp \alpha) = \{A \sim_\gamma \alpha\}$, by the marking-off identity, that $A \sim_\gamma \beta \sqsubseteq A \sim_\gamma \alpha$.

Next, we are going to show that $A \sim_\gamma \alpha \in \gamma(A \perp \beta)$. Let $X \in A \perp \beta$. Then it follows from $A \sim_\gamma \beta \in \gamma(A \perp \beta)$, again by the marking-off identity, that $X \sqsubseteq A \sim_\gamma \beta$. Since $\sqsubseteq$ is transitive, it follows from $X \sqsubseteq A \sim_\gamma \beta$ and $A \sim_\gamma \beta \sqsubseteq A \sim_\gamma \alpha$ that $X \sqsubseteq A \sim_\gamma \alpha$. We have shown that $X \sqsubseteq A \sim_\gamma \alpha$ for all $X \in A \perp \beta$, and since $A \sim_\gamma \alpha \in A \perp \beta$ it now follows by the marking-off identity that $A \sim_\gamma \alpha \in \gamma(A \perp \beta)$. It can be concluded from $A \sim_\gamma \alpha \in \gamma(A \perp \beta)$ and $\gamma(A \perp \beta) = \{A \sim_\gamma \beta\}$ that $A \sim_\gamma \alpha = A \sim_\gamma \beta$.

b. Let γ be as stated in the theorem, and let $A\sim_\gamma\alpha \nvdash \beta$ and $A\sim_\gamma\beta \nvdash \alpha$.

Case 1, $\alpha \notin A$: Then $A\sim_\gamma\alpha = A$. It follows from $A\sim_\gamma\alpha \nvdash \beta$ that $\beta \notin A$, which in its turn implies $A\sim_\gamma\beta = A$. We therefore have $A\sim_\gamma\alpha = A\sim_\gamma\beta = A$.

Case 2, $\beta \notin A$: Symmetrical with case 1.

Case 3, $\alpha \in A$ and $\beta \in A$: Since $\sim_\gamma$ is maxichoice, we have $A\sim_\gamma\alpha \in A\perp\alpha$. It follows from this, $\beta \in A$ and $\beta \notin A\sim_\gamma\alpha$, that $A\sim_\gamma\alpha \in A\perp\beta$. (Observation 1.53. Note that the logical closure of A is necessary here.) In the same way it follows that $A\sim_\gamma\beta \in A\perp\alpha$, and we can now use the result of Part *a* to obtain $A\sim_\gamma\alpha = A\sim_\gamma\beta$.

106. Let $\sqsubseteq$ be the transitive and weakly maximizing relation on which γ is based. Let $A\sim_\gamma(\alpha\&\beta) \vdash \alpha$. There are four cases.

Case 1, $\vdash\alpha$: It follows directly that $A\sim_\gamma(\alpha\&\beta\&\delta) \vdash \alpha$.

Case 2, $\vdash\beta$: Then $\alpha\&\beta$ and are logically equivalent, and consequently $A\sim_\gamma(\alpha\&\beta) = A\sim_\gamma\alpha$. From $A\sim_\gamma(\alpha\&\beta) \vdash \alpha$, i.e., $A\sim_\gamma\alpha \vdash \alpha$. it follows that $\alpha \in \mathrm{Cn}(\varnothing)$, and we are back in case 1.

Case 3, $\vdash\delta$: Then $\alpha\&\beta\&\delta$ is logically equivalent to $\alpha\&\beta$, so that $A\sim_\gamma(\alpha\&\beta\&\delta) = A\sim_\gamma(\alpha\&\beta)$, from which the desired result follows directly.

Case 4, $\nvdash\alpha$, $\nvdash\beta$ and $\nvdash\delta$: Let $\cap\gamma(A\perp(\alpha\&\beta)) \vdash \alpha$. We are first going to show that if $X \in \gamma(A\perp(\alpha\&\beta\&\delta))$, then $X \vdash \alpha$. Suppose not, i.e., suppose that there is some X such that $X \in \gamma(A\perp(\alpha\&\beta\&\delta))$ and $\alpha \notin \mathrm{Cn}(X)$. It follows from $X \in A\perp(\alpha\&\beta\&\delta)$ and $\alpha \notin \mathrm{Cn}(X)$ that $X \in A\perp(\alpha\&\beta)$.

Suppose that $X \in \gamma(A\perp(\alpha\&\beta))$. Then $\cap\gamma(A\perp(\alpha\&\beta)) \nvdash \alpha$, contrary to the conditions. By this contradiction, $X \notin \gamma(A\perp(\alpha\&\beta))$.

Next, let $Y \in \gamma(A\perp(\alpha\&\beta))$. Then $X \sqsubset Y$. Since $Y \nvdash \alpha\&\beta\&\delta$ there is, by the upper bound property, some Y' such that $Y \subseteq Y' \in A\perp(\alpha\&\beta\&\delta)$. If $Y = Y'$, then $X \sqsubset Y'$ follows directly from $X \sqsubset Y$. If $Y \subset Y'$, then the weak maximizing property yields $Y \sqsubseteq Y'$. It follows by transitivity from $X \sqsubset Y$ and $Y \sqsubseteq Y'$ that $X \sqsubset Y'$. In both cases, we have $X \sqsubset Y'$, $X \in \gamma(A\perp(\alpha\&\beta\&\delta))$ and $Y' \in A\perp(\alpha\&\beta\&\delta)$. This contradiction shows that $\alpha \notin \mathrm{Cn}(X)$ cannot hold. We can conclude that if $X \in \gamma(A\perp(\alpha\&\beta\&\delta))$, then $X \vdash \alpha$. Since $\gamma(A\perp(\alpha\&\beta\&\delta))$ has a finite number of elements, it follows by repeated application of Observation 1.34 that $\cap\gamma(A\perp(\alpha\&\beta\&\delta)) \vdash \alpha$. With this, the proof is finished.

107. a. Let $\sqsubseteq$ be the marking-off relation by which γ is relational. Let $\sqsubseteq'$ be the restriction of $\sqsubseteq$ to the domain $A\Delta\mathcal{L} = \{X \mid X \in A\perp\alpha \text{ for some } \alpha\}$. (Thus, if $X, Y \in A\Delta\mathcal{L}$, then $X\sqsubseteq'Y$ if and only if $X\sqsubseteq Y$, and otherwise $X\not\sqsubseteq'Y$.)

If $X, Y \in A\perp\alpha$, then $X\sqsubseteq Y$ if and only if $X\sqsubseteq'Y$. Therefore, it makes no difference to replace $\sqsubseteq$ by $\sqsubseteq'$ in the marking-off relation.

To see that $\sqsubseteq'$ is reflexive, let $X \in A\Delta\mathcal{L}$. It follows from Observation 1.70 that there is some β such that $\{X\} = A\perp\beta$. It follows from $\gamma(A\perp\beta) = A\perp\beta$, i.e., $\gamma(\{X\}) = \{X\}$, that $X\sqsubseteq X$ and thus $X\sqsubseteq'X$.

b. Suppose that $\sqsubseteq$ is transitive. To see that $\sqsubseteq'$ is transitive, let $X \sqsubseteq' Y \sqsubseteq' Z$. It follows that $X \sqsubseteq Y \sqsubseteq Z$, so that $X \sqsubseteq Z$. Since $X, Z \in A \Delta \mathcal{L}$, we then obtain $X \sqsubseteq' Z$.

108. a. Define $X < Y$ if and only if $\neg(Y \sqsubseteq X)$, and the two identities will be equivalent.
b. $X < Y \rightarrow \neg(Y < X)$
iff $\neg(Y \sqsubseteq X) \rightarrow \neg(\neg(X \sqsubseteq Y))$
iff $\neg(Y \sqsubseteq X) \rightarrow (X \sqsubseteq Y)$
iff $Y \sqsubseteq X \vee X \sqsubseteq Y$
c. Transitivity. Proof:
$X \sqsubseteq Z \rightarrow X \sqsubseteq Y \vee Y \sqsubseteq Z$
iff $\neg(Z < X) \rightarrow \neg(Y < X) \vee \neg(Z < Y)$
iff $\neg(\neg(Y < X) \vee \neg(Z < Y)) \rightarrow \neg(\neg(Z < X))$
iff $Y < X$ & $Z < Y \rightarrow Z < X$
iff $Z < Y$ & $Y < X \rightarrow Z < X$

109. Let the language consist of the logically independent atoms p and q and their truth-functional combinations, and let Cn represent classical truth-functional consequence. Let $A = \text{Cn}(\{p,q\})$. Then $A \perp \{p\} = \{\text{Cn}(\{q\}), \text{Cn}(\{p \leftrightarrow q\})\}$ and $A \perp \{p, p \leftrightarrow q\} = \{\text{Cn}(\{q\}), \text{Cn}(\{q \rightarrow p\})\}$. Let $\gamma(A \perp \{p\}) = \{\text{Cn}(\{q\})\}$ and $\gamma(A \perp \{p, p \leftrightarrow q\}) = \{\text{Cn}(\{q \rightarrow p\})\}$. If γ is relational by $\sqsubseteq$, then $\text{Cn}(\{p \leftrightarrow q\}) \sqsubset \text{Cn}(\{q\}) \sqsubset \text{Cn}(\{q \rightarrow p\})$. If $\sqsubseteq$ is transitive, then $\text{Cn}(\{p \leftrightarrow q\}) \sqsubset \text{Cn}(\{q \rightarrow p\})$. On the other hand, if $\sqsubseteq$ is maximizing, then $\text{Cn}(\{q \rightarrow p\}) \sqsubset \text{Cn}(\{p \leftrightarrow q\})$. Although $\sqsubseteq$ is transitively relational, it is not transitively, maximizingly relational.

110. a. Let B be an A-closed subset of A. Then, by Observation 1.67, there is a set X such that $\{B\} = A \perp X$. By Definition 2.61, $\gamma(A \perp X) = \{B\}$, and by the marking-off identity, $B \sqsubseteq B$, so that $\sqsubseteq$ is reflexive.
b. Let A_1 and A_2 be A-closed subsets of A such that neither of them is a proper subset of the other. Then, by Observation 1.68, there is a set X such that $\{A_1, A_2\} = A \perp X$. By Definition 2.61, either $A_1 \in \gamma(A \perp X)$ or $A_2 \in \gamma(A \perp X)$. By the marking-off identity, in the former case $A_2 \sqsubseteq A_1$ and in the latter $A_1 \sqsubseteq A_2$.
c. Let $\sqsubseteq'$ be defined as follows:

(I) If $A_1 \not\subset A_2 \not\subset A_1$, then $A_1 \sqsubseteq' A_2$ if and only if $A_1 \sqsubseteq A_2$

(II) If $A_1 \subset A_2$, then $A_1 \sqsubset' A_2$

We need to verify (1) that $\sqsubseteq'$ is connected, and (2) that $\sqsubseteq'$ generates the same partial meet contraction as $\sqsubseteq$.

(1) follows from the definition and Part *b*.

For (2), note that if $A_1, A_2 \in A \perp X$, then $A_1 \not\subset A_2 \not\subset A_1$, so that $A_1 \sqsubseteq' A_2$ holds if and only if $A_1 \sqsubseteq A_2$. Therefore, although $\sqsubseteq$ and $\sqsubseteq'$ do not necessarily coincide in general, it makes no difference to replace $\sqsubseteq$ by $\sqsubseteq'$ in the marking-off relation.

111. It follows directly from $A\perp\alpha \subseteq S(A,\alpha)$ that if $S(A,\alpha)$ is empty, then so is $A\perp\alpha$. For the other direction, let $A\perp\alpha = \varnothing$. Then $\vdash\alpha$, and it follows from clause (iii) of Definition 2.24 that $S(A,\alpha) = \varnothing$.

112. Suppose to the contrary that $S(A,\alpha) = S(A,\beta)$ and $A\perp\alpha \neq A\perp\beta$. Without loss of generality, we may assume that there is some X such that $X \in A\perp\alpha$ and $X \notin A\perp\beta$.

It follows from $X \in A\perp\alpha$ by Observation 2.23 that $X \in S(A,\alpha)$ and thus $X \in S(A,\beta)$, so that $\beta \notin X$. From this and $X \in A\perp\alpha$ it follows by Observation 1.53 that $X \in A\perp\beta$. This contradiction concludes the proof.

113. Let $\div$ be a maxichoice AGM-contraction that is based on the selection function γ. Let γ' be the selection function such that for all α, $\gamma'(S(A,\alpha)) = \gamma(A\perp\alpha)$. It follows from Exercise 112 that γ' is a well-defined selection function. Let $\div'$ be the Levi-contraction that is based on γ'. Then clearly $A\div\alpha = A\div'\alpha$ for all α.

114. *(1) implies (2)*: Let $Y \in S(A,\alpha)$. Then $Y = \text{Cn}(Y) \subseteq A$ and $Y \nvdash \alpha$. Let Z be any element of $A\perp\alpha$ such that $Y \subseteq Z$. It remains to be shown that $Z \cap \text{Cn}(\{\alpha\}) \subseteq Y$. Let $\varepsilon \in Z \cap \text{Cn}(\{\alpha\})$. Since $Y \in S(A,\alpha)$ we know that either ε or $\neg\varepsilon$ is an element of $\text{Cn}(Y\cup \{\neg\alpha\})$.

If $\neg\varepsilon \in \text{Cn}(Y\cup \{\neg\alpha\})$, then since $Y \subseteq Z$ we have $\neg\varepsilon \in \text{Cn}(Z\cup \{\neg\alpha\})$, and by deduction $\neg\alpha\rightarrow\neg\varepsilon \in \text{Cn}(Z)$. Since $\varepsilon \in Z$ this implies $\alpha \in \text{Cn}(Z)$, contrary to $Z \in A\perp\alpha$. We can conclude from this contradiction that $\neg\varepsilon \notin \text{Cn}(Y\cup \{\neg\alpha\})$, and thus $\varepsilon \in \text{Cn}(Y\cup \{\neg\alpha\})$.

By deduction, $\neg\alpha\rightarrow\varepsilon \in \text{Cn}(Y)$. Since $\varepsilon \in Z \cap \text{Cn}(\{\alpha\})$, deduction also yields $\alpha\rightarrow\varepsilon \in \text{Cn}(\varnothing)$ and thus $\alpha\rightarrow\varepsilon \in \text{Cn}(Y)$. Since ε can be derived from $\neg\alpha\rightarrow\varepsilon$ and $\alpha\rightarrow\varepsilon$, we obtain $\varepsilon \in \text{Cn}(Y)$, hence $\varepsilon \in Y$. This finishes the proof.

(2) implies (3): Since $Y \subseteq A$ and $Y \nvdash \alpha$ it follows from the upper bound property that that there is some Z such that $Y \subseteq Z \in A\perp\alpha$. It follows from (2) that then $Z \cap \text{Cn}(\{\alpha\}) \subseteq Y$ also holds.

(3) implies (1): Let Y be logically closed, and let $Z \cap \text{Cn}(\{\alpha\}) \subseteq Y \subseteq Z \in A\perp\alpha$. It follows directly that clauses (i) and (ii) of Definition 2.24 are satisfied. It remains to be shown that clause (iii) is satisfied, in other words that $\text{Cn}(Y \cup \{\neg\alpha\}) \in \mathcal{L}\perp\perp$. It follows from $Z \in A\perp\alpha$ that $\text{Cn}(Z\cup \{\neg\alpha\}) \in \mathcal{L}\perp\perp$ (Observation 2.23), so it will be sufficient to show that $\text{Cn}(Y\cup \{\neg\alpha\}) = \text{Cn}(Z\cup \{\neg\alpha\})$.

Since $Y \subseteq Z$ we immediately have $\text{Cn}(Y\cup \{\neg\alpha\}) \subseteq \text{Cn}(Z\cup \{\neg\alpha\})$. In order to show that $\text{Cn}(Z\cup \{\neg\alpha\}) \subseteq \text{Cn}(Y\cup \{\neg\alpha\}$, let $\delta \in \text{Cn}(Z\cup \{\neg\alpha\})$.

Then by deduction $\neg\alpha\rightarrow\delta \in \text{Cn}(Z)$, i.e., since Z is logically closed, $\neg\alpha\rightarrow\delta \in Z$. Since $\neg\alpha\rightarrow\delta \in \text{Cn}(\{\alpha\})$, we have $\neg\alpha\rightarrow\delta \in Z \cap \text{Cn}(\{\alpha\})$. Since $Z \cap \text{Cn}(\{\alpha\}) \subseteq Y$ we may conclude that $\neg\alpha\rightarrow\delta \in Y$ and thus, by deduction, $\delta \in \text{Cn}(Y \cup \{\neg\alpha\})$.

115. a. Using the result from the foregoing exercise we obtain:
$A+\alpha = \cap(S(A,\alpha))$
$= \cap\{Y \mid Z \cap \text{Cn}(\{\alpha\}) \subseteq Y = \text{Cn}(Y) \subseteq Z \in A\bot\alpha \text{ for some } Z\}$
$= \cap\{Y \mid \text{Cn}(Z \cap \text{Cn}(\{\alpha\})) \subseteq Y = \text{Cn}(Y) \subseteq Z \in A\bot\alpha \text{ for some } Z\}$
$= \cap\{\text{Cn}(Z \cap \text{Cn}(\{\alpha\})) \mid Z \in A\bot\alpha\}$
$= \cap\{Z \cap \text{Cn}(\{\alpha\}) \mid Z \in A\bot\alpha\}$
$= \cap(A\bot\alpha) \cap \text{Cn}(\{\alpha\})$
$= (A{\sim}\alpha) \cap \text{Cn}(\{\alpha\})$
b. $A+\alpha = (A{\sim}\alpha) \cap \text{Cn}(\{\alpha\})$ (Part *a* of this exercise)
$= A \cap \text{Cn}(\{\neg\alpha\}) \cap \text{Cn}(\{\alpha\})$ (Observation 2.12)
$= A \cap \text{Cn}(\{\neg\alpha\vee\alpha\})$ (Observation 1.17)
$= A \cap \text{Cn}(\varnothing)$
$= \text{Cn}(\varnothing)$.

116. a. $A \perp\!\!\!\perp p = \{\{p\}\}$
b. $A \perp\!\!\!\perp (p\vee q) = \{\{p\},\{q\},\{p\vee q\}\}$
c. $A \perp\!\!\!\perp (p\&q) = \{\{p,q\}\}$
d. $A \perp\!\!\!\perp (p\rightarrow q) = \{\{q\}\}$
e. $A \perp\!\!\!\perp (p\vee\neg p) = \{\varnothing\}$
f. $A \perp\!\!\!\perp (p\&\neg p) = \varnothing$

117. a. $(\text{Cn}(A)) \perp\!\!\!\perp p = \{\{p\}, \{p\&q\}, \{p\leftrightarrow q,q\}, \{p\leftrightarrow q,p\vee q\}, \{q,q\rightarrow p\}, \{p\vee q,q\rightarrow p\}\}$
b. $(\text{Cn}(A)) \perp\!\!\!\perp (p\vee q) = \{\{p\},\{p\&q\},\{q\},\{p\vee q\}\}$
c. $(\text{Cn}(A)) \perp\!\!\!\perp (p\vee\neg p) = \{\varnothing\}$
d. $(\text{Cn}(A)) \perp\!\!\!\perp (p\&\neg p) = \varnothing$

118. a. Let $A \subseteq B$ and $X \in A \perp\!\!\!\perp \alpha$. Then $X \subseteq B$, and X implies α but none of its proper subsets implies α. It follows that $X \in B \perp\!\!\!\perp \alpha$.
b. Let $X \in B \perp\!\!\!\perp \alpha \cap \wp(A)$. $X \in \wp(A)$ is equivalent with $X \subseteq A$. Thus $X \subseteq A$, and X implies α but none of its proper subsets implies α. It follows that $X \in A \perp\!\!\!\perp \beta$.
c. One direction follows from Part *b*. For the other direction, let $A \subseteq B$ and $X \in A \perp\!\!\!\perp \alpha$. Then $X \in B \perp\!\!\!\perp \alpha$ follows from Part *a*. It follows from $X \in A \perp\!\!\!\perp \alpha$ that $X \subseteq A$, or equivalently $X \in \wp(A)$.
d. For one direction, let $X \in A \perp\!\!\!\perp \alpha$. It follows directly that $X \subseteq A$, and by Part *b* of this exercise that $X \in X \perp\!\!\!\perp \alpha$.

For the other direction, suppose that $X \subseteq A$ and $X \in X \perp\!\!\perp \alpha$. It follows by Part *a* of the present exercise that $X \in A \perp\!\!\perp \alpha$.
e. Suppose to the contrary that $\delta \in X \in A \perp\!\!\perp \alpha$ and $X \setminus \{\delta\} \vdash \delta$. Then $\text{Cn}(X \setminus \{\delta\}) = \text{Cn}(X)$, and $X \setminus \{\delta\}$ is a proper subset of X that implies α, contrary to $X \in A \perp\!\!\perp \alpha$.
f. Let $X \in (A \perp\!\!\perp \alpha) \cap (A \perp\!\!\perp \beta)$. Then (i) $X \subseteq A$, (ii) X implies $\alpha \& \beta$, and (iii) no proper subset of X implies α, so that no proper subset of X implies $\alpha \& \beta$. We can conclude that $X \in A \perp\!\!\perp (\alpha \& \beta)$.
g. Let $X \subseteq Y$, $X \in A \perp\!\!\perp \alpha$, and $Y \in A \perp\!\!\perp \beta$. Then (i) $Y \subseteq A$, (ii) Y implies $\alpha \& \beta$, and (iii) no proper subset of Y implies β, so that no proper subset of Y implies $\alpha \& \beta$. We can conclude that $Y \in A \perp\!\!\perp (\alpha \& \beta)$.

119. We first need to show that $Z \vdash \delta \vee \alpha$. Let $Y = \{\psi_1, \ldots \psi_n\}$. Then $Z = \{\delta \vee \psi_1, \ldots \delta \vee \psi_n\}$, and thus $Z \vdash \delta \vee (\psi_1 \& \ldots \& \psi_n)$. It follows by sentential logic from this and $(\psi_1 \& \ldots \& \psi_n) \vdash \delta \vee \alpha$ that $Z \vdash \delta \vee \alpha$.

Next, suppose that $Z \notin A \perp\!\!\perp (\delta \vee \alpha)$. Then there is some proper subset Z' of Z such that $Z' \vdash \delta \vee \alpha$. It follows from the construction of Z that there is some proper subset Y' of Y such that $Z' = \{\delta \vee \psi \mid \psi \in Y'\}$. Since Z' is logically equivalent with $\delta \vee \& Y'$, we then have $(\delta \vee \& Y') \vdash \delta \vee \alpha$. From this it follows truth-functionally that $\& Y' \vdash \delta \vee \alpha$, so that $Y' \vdash \delta \vee \alpha$, contrary to $Y' \subset Y$ and $Y \in A \perp\!\!\perp (\delta \vee \alpha)$. We can conclude from this contradiction that $Z \in A \perp\!\!\perp (\delta \vee \alpha)$.

120. *Maxichoice to unicity*: Let $\approx_\sigma$ be a maxichoice contraction, i.e., let there be a maxichoice selection function γ for A such that $A \sim_\gamma \alpha = A \approx_\sigma \alpha$ for all α. Let $\beta \in \sigma(A \perp\!\!\perp \alpha)$.

We then have $\beta \in A \setminus (A \approx_\sigma \alpha) = A \setminus (A \sim_\gamma \alpha)$. Since γ is maxichoice, we have $A \sim_\gamma \alpha \in A \perp \alpha$, so that $(A \sim_\gamma \alpha) \cup \{\beta\} \vdash \alpha$.

Using compactness, we can conclude from $(A \sim_\gamma \alpha) \cup \{\beta\} \vdash \alpha$ that there is a finite set Z such that $Z \subseteq A \sim_\gamma \alpha$ and $Z \cup \{\beta\} \vdash \alpha$. There must then be some $Z' \subseteq Z$ such that $Z' \cup \{\beta\} \in A \perp\!\!\perp \alpha$.

It follows from $Z' \subseteq Z \subseteq A \sim_\gamma \alpha = A \approx_\sigma \alpha = A \setminus (\sigma(A \perp\!\!\perp \alpha))$ that $Z' \cap \sigma(A \perp\!\!\perp \alpha) = \varnothing$. Thus, we have $Z' \cup \{\beta\} \in A \perp\!\!\perp \alpha$ and $(Z' \cup \{\beta\}) \cap \sigma(A \perp\!\!\perp \alpha) = \{\beta\}$, which concludes this direction of the proof.

Unicity to maxichoice: Let σ be such that for all $\beta \in \sigma(A \perp\!\!\perp \alpha)$ there is some $X \in A \perp\!\!\perp \alpha$ such that $X \cap \sigma(A \perp\!\!\perp \alpha) = \{\beta\}$.

In order to show that $\approx_\sigma$ is a maxichoice contraction, it is sufficient to show that for all α, $A \approx_\sigma \alpha \in A \perp \alpha$. This can be shown by proving that if $\beta \in A \setminus (A \approx_\sigma \alpha)$, then $(A \approx_\sigma \alpha) \cup \{\beta\} \vdash \alpha$.

Let $\beta \in A \setminus (A \approx_\sigma \alpha)$. Then $\beta \in \sigma(A \perp\!\!\perp \alpha)$. It follows by unicity that there is some $X \in A \perp\!\!\perp \alpha$ such that $X \cap \sigma(A \perp\!\!\perp \alpha) = \{\beta\}$. Since $X \subseteq A$ it follows set-theoretically from $X \cap \sigma(A \perp\!\!\perp \alpha) = \{\beta\}$ that $X \subseteq (A \setminus \sigma(A \perp\!\!\perp \alpha)) \cup \{\beta\} =$

$(A{\approx_\sigma}\alpha)\cup\{\beta\}$. It follows from $X \in A{\perp\!\!\perp}\alpha$ that $X \vdash \alpha$, and we can conclude that $(A{\approx_\sigma}\alpha)\cup\{\beta\} \vdash \alpha$, as desired.

121. a. We are going to assume that $A{\approx_\sigma}\alpha \neq A{\approx_\sigma}\beta$, and show that there is some δ for which it does not hold that $A{\approx_\sigma}\delta \vdash \alpha$ iff $A{\approx_\sigma}\delta \vdash \beta$.

It follows from $A{\approx_\sigma}\alpha \neq A{\approx_\sigma}\beta$ that $A{\perp\!\!\perp}\alpha \neq A{\perp\!\!\perp}\beta$. By Observation 2.84, $A\perp\alpha \neq A\perp\beta$. Without loss of generality we may assume that there is some $X \in A\perp\alpha$ such that $X \notin A\perp\beta$. There are two cases:

Case 1, $X \vdash \beta$: Since $X \in A\perp\alpha$ we can use Observation 1.70 to conclude that there is some δ such that $\{X\} = A\perp\delta$. By Observation 2.86, every element of $A{\perp\!\!\perp}\delta$ has exactly one element. Thus $A{\approx_\sigma}\delta = A\backslash\cup(A{\perp\!\!\perp}\delta)$. It follows from Observation 2.85 that $A\backslash\cup(A{\perp\!\!\perp}\delta) = \cap(A\perp\delta) = X$. We therefore have $A{\approx_\sigma}\delta = X$, so that $A{\approx_\sigma}\delta \nvdash \alpha$ and $A{\approx_\sigma}\delta \vdash \beta$, as desired.

Case 2, $X \nvdash \beta$. Then, since A is finite, there is some X' such that $X \subset X' \in A\perp\beta$. It follows in the same way as in case 1 that there is some δ such that $A{\approx_\sigma}\delta = X'$. It follows that $A{\approx_\sigma}\delta \vdash \alpha$ and $A{\approx_\sigma}\delta \nvdash \beta$.

b. Let $A{\approx_\sigma}\beta \not\subseteq A{\approx_\sigma}\alpha$. It follows that $A{\approx_\sigma}\alpha \neq A$, so that $\nvdash \alpha$. It also follows that there is some ε such that $\varepsilon \in \sigma(A{\perp\!\!\perp}\alpha)$ and $\varepsilon \notin \sigma(A{\perp\!\!\perp}\beta)$. By Definition 2.30, $\varepsilon \in \cup(A{\perp\!\!\perp}\alpha)$, and according to Observation 2.85, $\varepsilon \notin \cap(A\perp\alpha)$. Let X be such that $\varepsilon \notin X \in A\perp\alpha$. By Observation 1.70, there is some δ such that $\{X\} = A\perp\delta$. By Observation 2.86, every element of $A{\perp\!\!\perp}\delta$ has exactly one element, and consequently $\sigma(A{\perp\!\!\perp}\delta) = \cup(A{\perp\!\!\perp}\delta)$ and $A{\approx_\sigma}\delta = A\backslash\cup(A{\perp\!\!\perp}\delta)$. By Observation 2.85, $A{\approx_\sigma}\delta = \cap(A\perp\delta) = X$.

It follows from $\varepsilon \in A$ and $\varepsilon \notin X \in A\perp\alpha$ that $X \cup \{\varepsilon\} \vdash \alpha$. Since $\varepsilon \in A{\approx_\sigma}\beta$, we therefore have $A{\approx_\sigma}\delta \nvdash \alpha$ and $(A{\approx_\sigma}\beta) \cup (A{\approx_\sigma}\delta) \vdash \alpha$, as desired.

122. a. Let $\alpha{\prec\!\!\cdot}\beta$ and $\beta{\vdash}\delta$. Then either $\beta{\leftrightarrow}\delta \in \mathrm{Cn}(\varnothing)$ or $\mathrm{Cn}(\delta) \subset \mathrm{Cn}(\beta)$. In the former case, $\alpha{\prec\!\!\cdot}\delta$ follows from intersubstitutivity (Definition 2.43). In the latter case, strict dominance yields $\beta{\prec\!\!\cdot}\delta$, and $\alpha{\prec\!\!\cdot}\delta$ can be obtained from transitivity.

b. Let $\alpha{\vdash}\beta$ and $\beta{\prec\!\!\cdot}\delta$. Then either $\alpha{\leftrightarrow}\beta \in \mathrm{Cn}(\varnothing)$ or $\mathrm{Cn}(\beta) \subset \mathrm{Cn}(\alpha)$. In the former case, $\alpha{\prec\!\!\cdot}\delta$ follows from intersubstitutivity (Definition 2.43). In the latter case, strict dominance yields $\alpha{\prec\!\!\cdot}\beta$, and $\alpha{\prec\!\!\cdot}\delta$ can be obtained from transitivity.

123. Let ${\prec\!\!\cdot}$ be a hierarchy that satisfies virtual connectivity, and let $\alpha{\prec\!\!\cdot}\beta$ and $\beta{\prec\!\!\cdot}\delta$. It follows from virtual connectivity that either $\alpha{\prec\!\!\cdot}\delta$ or $\delta{\prec\!\!\cdot}\beta$. In the latter case, acyclicity is violated. We can conclude that $\alpha{\prec\!\!\cdot}\delta$.

124. a. *Closure*: It follows from $A{+}\alpha = \mathrm{Cn}(A\backslash\sigma(A{\perp\!\!\perp}\alpha))$ that $\mathrm{Cn}(A{+}\alpha) = \mathrm{Cn}(\mathrm{Cn}(A\backslash\sigma(A{\perp\!\!\perp}\alpha))) = \mathrm{Cn}(A\backslash\sigma(A{\perp\!\!\perp}\alpha)) = A{+}\alpha$.

Inclusion: It follows from $A\backslash\sigma(A\perp\!\!\perp\alpha) \subseteq A$ that $\text{Cn}(A\backslash\sigma(A\perp\!\!\perp\alpha)) \subseteq \text{Cn}(A)$, i.e. (since A is logically closed) $A+\alpha \subseteq A$.
Vacuity: If $\alpha \notin \text{Cn}(A)$, then $A\perp\!\!\perp\alpha = \varnothing$ so that $\sigma(A\perp\!\!\perp\alpha) = \varnothing$ and consequently $\text{Cn}(A\backslash\sigma(A\perp\!\!\perp\alpha)) = \text{Cn}(A) = A$.
Success: Let B be any subset of A that implies α. Then $B \not\subseteq A\backslash\sigma(A\perp\!\!\perp\alpha))$. It follows from this that $A\backslash\sigma(A\perp\!\!\perp\alpha))$ does not imply α, and thus $\alpha \notin \text{Cn}(A\backslash\sigma(A\perp\!\!\perp\alpha))$.
Extensionality: Directly from the intersubstitutivity of the hierarchy $\prec$. (Definition 2.43.)
b. *Failure*: Let $\tau \in \text{Cn}(\varnothing)$. Then $\tau \in A$. Let α be any element of A. Then $\{\alpha\} \in A\perp\!\!\perp\tau$, and consequently $\alpha \in s(\{\alpha\}) \subseteq \sigma(A\perp\!\!\perp\tau)$. It follows that $\sigma(A\perp\!\!\perp\tau) = A$, and consequently $A+\tau = \text{Cn}(A\backslash\sigma(A\perp\!\!\perp\tau)) = \text{Cn}(\varnothing)$, contrary to *failure*.
c. Suppose that *recovery* is satisfied. It then follows from Part *a* and Observations 2.6 and 2.3 that *failure* is satisfied, contrary to Part *b*. We can conclude that *recovery* does not hold.

125. Suppose to the contrary that $\delta \in \sigma(A\perp\!\!\perp\alpha)$ and $\delta \in \text{Cn}(\{\neg\alpha\})$. There is then some $X \in A\perp\!\!\perp\alpha$ such that $\delta \in s(X)$.

Let $Y = X\backslash\{\delta\}$. It follows from $Y\cup\{\delta\} \vdash \alpha$ by the deduction property that $Y \vdash \delta\rightarrow\alpha$. It follows from $\delta \in \text{Cn}(\{\neg\alpha\})$ that $\neg\alpha\rightarrow\delta \in \text{Cn}(\varnothing)$ or equivalently $\neg\delta\rightarrow\alpha \in \text{Cn}(\varnothing)$. Since $\delta\rightarrow\alpha$ and $\neg\delta\rightarrow\alpha$ together imply α we have $Y \vdash \alpha$. Since $Y \subset X$ this contradicts $X \in A\perp\!\!\perp\alpha$. This contradiction concludes the proof.

126. *Left-to-right*: Let $\delta \in A\backslash\sigma(A\perp\!\!\perp\alpha)$. If $\delta \in \text{Cn}(\{\neg\alpha\})$, then clearly $\delta \in A\cap\text{Cn}(\{\neg\alpha\})$. If $\delta \notin \text{Cn}(\{\neg\alpha\})$, then it follows from Observation 2.90 that $\delta \notin \sigma(A\perp\!\!\perp\alpha)$, and thus $\delta \in A\backslash\sigma(A\perp\!\!\perp\alpha)$.

Right-to-left: It follows from $A\perp\!\!\perp\alpha \subseteq A\perp\!\!\perp\alpha$ that $\sigma(A\perp\!\!\perp\alpha) \subseteq \sigma(A\perp\!\!\perp\alpha)$ and consequently $A\backslash\sigma(A\perp\!\!\perp\alpha) \subseteq A\backslash\sigma(A\perp\!\!\perp\alpha)$. It follows from Exercise 125 that $A\cap\text{Cn}(\{\neg\alpha\}) \subseteq A\backslash\sigma(A\perp\!\!\perp\alpha)$.

127. Since $\prec$ is empty, all elements of all kernels are minimal, i.e., $s(X) = X$ for all $X \in A\perp\!\!\perp\alpha$. It follows that $\sigma(A\perp\!\!\perp\alpha) = \cup(A\perp\!\!\perp\alpha)$, and thus $A+\alpha = \text{Cn}(A\backslash\sigma(A\perp\!\!\perp\alpha)) = \text{Cn}(A\backslash\cup(A\perp\!\!\perp\alpha))$. According to Observation 2.85, $A\backslash\cup(A\perp\!\!\perp\alpha)) = \cap(A\perp\alpha)$, and thus $A+\alpha = \text{Cn}(\cap(A\perp\alpha))$. Since $\cap(A\perp\alpha)$ is logically closed, we therefore have $A+\alpha = \cap(A\perp\alpha)$, as desired.

128. a. From $\alpha\vdash\alpha$ and *dominance*.
b. From Part *a* and *intersubstitutivity* (Observation 2.92).
c. For one direction, let $\alpha\leq\beta$. By *conjunctiveness*, either $\alpha\leq\alpha\&\beta$ or $\beta\leq\alpha\&\beta$. In the first case, we are done, and in the second case, we can apply *transitivity* to $\alpha\leq\beta$ and $\beta\leq\alpha\&\beta$ to obtain $\alpha\leq\alpha\&\beta$.

For the other direction, let $\alpha\leq\alpha\&\beta$. We can apply *dominance* to obtain $\alpha\&\beta\leq\beta$ an then *transitivity* to obtain $\alpha\leq\beta$.
d. Let $\alpha\leq\beta$. It follows from *dominance* that $\alpha\&\delta\leq\alpha$, and then from *transitivity* that $\alpha\&\delta\leq\beta$.
e. Let $\alpha\leq\beta$. It follows from *dominance* that $\alpha\&\delta\leq\alpha$ and $\beta\leq\beta\vee\varepsilon$. We can apply *transitivity* to $\alpha\&\delta\leq\alpha\leq\beta\leq\beta\vee\varepsilon$ and obtain $\alpha\&\delta\leq\beta\vee\varepsilon$.
f. By *conjunctiveness*, either $\alpha\leq\alpha\&\beta$ or $\beta\leq\alpha\&\beta$. In the first case, we can apply *transitivity* to $\delta\leq\alpha$ and $\alpha\leq\alpha\&\beta$ and obtain $\delta\leq\alpha\&\beta$. In the second case, we instead apply *transitivity* to $\delta\leq\beta$ and $\beta\leq\alpha\&\beta$, obtaining $\delta\leq\alpha\&\beta$ in this case as well.
g. Suppose to the contrary that $\alpha\leq\beta$ and $\neg(\alpha\&\delta\leq\beta\&\delta)$. From *connectivity* (Observation 2.48) we obtain $\beta\&\delta<\alpha\&\delta$. Due to *conjunctiveness*, either $\beta\leq\beta\&\delta$ or $\delta\leq\beta\&\delta$.

If $\beta\leq\beta\&\delta$, then we can apply *transitivity* and Observation 2.75 to $\alpha\leq\beta\leq\beta\&\delta<\alpha\&\delta$ and obtain $\alpha<\alpha\&\delta$ and thus $\neg(\alpha\&\delta\leq\alpha)$, contrary to *dominance*. If $\delta\leq\beta\&\delta$, then we can apply *transitivity* and Observation 2.75 to $\delta\leq\beta\&\delta<\alpha\&\delta$ and obtain $\delta<\alpha\&\delta$ and thus $\neg(\alpha\&\delta\leq\delta)$, again contrary to *dominance*. These contradictions conclude the proof.

129. a. Let $\alpha<\beta$. By *dominance*, $\alpha\&\beta\leq\alpha$. Applying *transitivity* (and Observation 2.75) we obtain $\alpha\&\beta<\beta$.
b. Let $\alpha<\beta$. It follows from *dominance* that $\alpha\&\delta\leq\alpha$. We can apply *transitivity* and Observation 2.75 to $\alpha\&\delta\leq\alpha<\beta$ and obtain $\alpha\&\delta<\beta$.
c. Let $\alpha<\beta$. It follows from *dominance* that $\beta\leq\beta\vee\delta$. We can apply *transitivity* and Observation 2.75 to $\alpha<\beta\leq\beta\vee\delta$ and obtain $\alpha<\beta\vee\delta$.
d. Let $\alpha<\beta$.It follows from *dominance* that $\alpha\&\delta\leq\alpha$ and $\beta\leq\beta\vee\varepsilon$. We can apply *transitivity* and Observation 2.75 to $\alpha\&\delta\leq\alpha<\beta\leq\beta\vee\varepsilon$ and obtain $\alpha\&\delta<\beta\vee\varepsilon$.
e. Let $\alpha\&\beta<\beta$. By *conjunctiveness*, either $\alpha\leq\alpha\&\beta$ or $\beta\leq\alpha\&\beta$. However, $\beta\leq\alpha\&\beta$ cannot hold, since $\alpha\&\beta<\beta$. Thus, $\alpha\leq\alpha\&\beta$. It follows from this and $\alpha\&\beta<\beta$, by *transitivity* and Observation 2.75, that $\alpha<\beta$.
f. It follows by *dominance* from $\beta\&\delta\vdash\alpha$ that $\beta\&\delta\leq\alpha$. By *transitivity* and Observation 2.75, $\beta\&\delta\leq\alpha$ and $\alpha<\beta$ yield $\beta\&\delta<\beta$.

It follows from conjunctiveness that either $\beta\leq\beta\&\delta$ or $\delta\leq\beta\&\delta$. Since we have just shown that $\beta\&\delta<\beta$, we can conclude that $\delta\leq\beta\&\delta$. It follows from $\delta\leq\beta\&\delta$ and $\beta\&\delta<\beta$, again with the help of *transitivity* and Observation 2.75, that $\delta<\beta$.
g. Let $\beta\&\delta<\alpha$. Suppose, to the contrary, that $\neg(\beta<\alpha)$ and $\neg(\delta<\alpha)$. From *connectivity* (Observation 2.48) we obtain $\alpha\leq\beta$ and $\alpha\leq\delta$. Due to *conjunctiveness*, either $\beta\leq\beta\&\delta$ or $\delta\leq\beta\&\delta$. In the first case, we can apply *transitivity* to $\alpha\leq\beta\leq\beta\&\delta$ to obtain $\alpha\leq\beta\&\delta$. In the second case, we can apply *transitivity* to $\alpha\leq\delta\leq\beta\&\delta$ to obtain $\alpha\leq\beta\&\delta$. Since $\alpha\leq\beta\&\delta$ contradicts $\beta\&\delta<\alpha$, we are done.

h. Let $\alpha\&\delta<\beta\&\delta$. By *conjunctiveness*, either $\alpha\leq\alpha\&\delta$ or $\delta\leq\alpha\&\delta$. Suppose that $\delta\leq\alpha\&\delta$. We then have $\delta\leq\alpha\&\delta$, $\alpha\&\delta<\beta\&\delta$, and (by *dominance*) $\beta\&\delta\leq\delta$. It follows by *transitivity* and Observation 2.75 that $\delta<\delta$, which is impossible. Thus not $\delta\leq\alpha\&\delta$, thus $\alpha\leq\alpha\&\delta$.

We thus have $\alpha\leq\alpha\&\delta$, $\alpha\&\delta<\beta\&\delta$, and (by *dominance*) $\beta\&\delta\leq\beta$. Again using *transitivity* and Observation 2.75 we obtain $\alpha<\beta$.

i. Let $\alpha<\beta$ and $\delta<\varepsilon$. It follows from *conjunctiveness* that either $\beta\leq\beta\&\varepsilon$ or $\varepsilon\leq\beta\&\varepsilon$.

If $\beta\leq\beta\&\varepsilon$, then we have $\alpha\&\delta\leq\alpha$ (by *dominance*), $\alpha<\beta$, and $\beta\leq\beta\&\varepsilon$. It follows by *transitivity* and Observation 2.75 that $\alpha\&\delta<\beta\&\varepsilon$.

If $\varepsilon\leq\beta\&\varepsilon$, then we can in the same way obtain $\alpha\&\delta\leq\delta$, $\delta<\varepsilon$, and $\varepsilon\leq\beta\&\varepsilon$. Again, we obtain $\alpha\&\delta<\beta\&\varepsilon$.

j. For one direction, let $\neg\alpha < \alpha\rightarrow\beta$. It follows from *conjunctiveness* and intersubstitutivity (Observation 2.92) that either $\alpha\rightarrow\neg\beta\leq\neg\alpha$ or $\alpha\rightarrow\beta\leq\neg\alpha$. The latter cannot hold, since $\neg\alpha < \alpha\rightarrow\beta$. Thus, $\alpha\rightarrow\neg\beta\leq\neg\alpha$. It follows by *transitivity* and Observation 2.75 that $\alpha\rightarrow\neg\beta < \alpha\rightarrow\beta$.

For the other direction, let $\alpha\rightarrow\neg\beta < \alpha\rightarrow\beta$. It follows from *dominance* that $\neg\alpha\leq\alpha\rightarrow\neg\beta$. We can use *transitivity* and Observation 2.75 to obtain $\neg\alpha < \alpha\rightarrow\beta$. This concludes the proof.

130. Since $\vdash\alpha$, it holds for all sentences δ that $\delta\vdash\alpha$ and (due to *dominance*) that $\delta\leq\alpha$. We can use *transitivity* to conclude that $\delta\leq\beta$ for all δ, and then *maximality* to conclude that $\vdash\beta$.

131. It follows from *connectivity* that $\alpha\leq\alpha$. It also follows from *connectivity* that either $\alpha\leq\beta$ or $\beta\leq\alpha$.

If $\alpha\leq\beta$, then we have $\alpha\leq\alpha$ and $\alpha\leq\beta$, and the condition given in the exercise can be used to derive $\alpha\leq\alpha\&\beta$.

If $\beta\leq\alpha$, then $\beta\leq\alpha\&\beta$ follows in the same way.

132. a. To be a hierarchy, < must satisfy *acyclicity* and *intersubstitutivity*. The latter follows from Observation 2.92. For *acyclicity*, suppose that $\alpha_1<\ldots<\alpha_n$. It follows from transitivity that $\alpha_1\leq\alpha_n$, and from this that $\alpha_n<\alpha_1$ does not hold.

b. Let $\alpha<\beta$ and $\beta\vdash\delta$. It follows from *dominance* that $\beta\leq\delta$ and from *transitivity* and Observation 2.75 that $\alpha<\delta$.

c. Let $\alpha\vdash\beta$ and $\beta<\delta$. It follows from *dominance* that $\alpha\leq\beta$ and from *transitivity* and Observation 2.75 that $\alpha<\delta$.

d. This can be shown by proving that if the right-hand side of the implication does not hold, then neither does the left-hand side. Suppose that neither $\alpha<\delta$ nor $\delta<\beta$. Then by *connectivity* (Observation 2.48), $\delta\leq\alpha$ and $\beta\leq\delta$. By *transitivity*, $\beta\leq\alpha$, and thus not $\alpha<\beta$.

133. a. EE1: Since $\top \vdash \top$ it follows from dominance that $\top \leq \top$, hence $\neg(\top < \top)$.
EE2↑, EE2↓, EE3↑, and EE3↓: See Exercise 132, parts b and c, and Exercise 129, parts i and e.

b. *Dominance*: Suppose to the contrary that there are sentences α and β such that $\alpha \vdash \beta$ and $\neg(\alpha \leq \beta)$. We then have $\beta < \alpha$, and EE2↑ yields $\alpha < \alpha$.

It can be shown, however, that $\alpha < \alpha$ does not hold. Suppose for contradiction that $\alpha < \alpha$. Since $\top \& \alpha \vdash \alpha$, we can then use EE2↓ to obtain $\top \& \alpha < \alpha$, and EE3↓ yields $\top < \alpha$. Since $\alpha \vdash \top$, we can use EE2↑ to obtain $\top < \top$, contrary to EE1. This contradiction concludes the proof.

Conjunctiveness. Suppose to the contrary that $\neg(\alpha \leq \alpha \& \beta)$ and $\neg(\beta \leq \alpha \& \beta)$. Then $\alpha \& \beta < \alpha$ and $\alpha \& \beta < \beta$. We can use EE3↑ to obtain $\alpha \& \beta < \alpha \& \beta$, contrary to the irreflexivity of < (that was shown in Part *a* of this exercise).

c. EE↑ implies EE2↑: Let $B = \{\beta\}$.
EE↑ implies EE3↑: $B = \{\beta, \delta\}$
EE2↑ and EE3↑ imply EE↑: Let α and B be such that $\alpha < \beta$ for all $\beta \in B$, and let $B \vdash \delta$. It follows from compactness that there is a finite subset $\{\beta_1, ... \beta_n\}$ of B such that $\{\beta_1, ... \beta_n\} \vdash \delta$. Repeated application of EE3↑ yields $\alpha < \beta_1 \& ... \& \beta_n$. We can use EE2↑ to obtain $\alpha < \delta$.

d. EE↓ implies EE2↓: If $\alpha \vdash \beta$, then $\{\alpha, \delta\} \vdash \beta$. The conclusion follows directly.
EE↓ implies EE3↓: Let $\alpha \& \beta < \beta$. Clearly, $\{\alpha, \beta\} \vdash \alpha \& \beta$. We can apply EE↓ to $\{\alpha, \beta\} \vdash \alpha \& \beta$ and $\alpha \& \beta < \beta$, and obtain $\alpha < \beta$.
EE2↓ and EE3↓ imply EE↓: Let $\{\alpha, \delta\} \vdash \beta$ and $\beta < \delta$. Since $\delta \& (\delta \rightarrow \beta) \vdash \beta$ and $\beta < \delta$, we can use EE2↓ to obtain $\delta \& (\delta \rightarrow \beta) < \delta$, and then EE3↓ to obtain $\delta \rightarrow \beta < \delta$. It follows from $\{\alpha, \delta\} \vdash \beta$ that $\alpha \vdash \delta \rightarrow \beta$. We therefore have $\alpha \vdash \delta \rightarrow \beta$ and $\delta \rightarrow \beta < \delta$, and EE2↓ yields $\alpha < \delta$.

134. For one direction, let $\alpha \in A$. It follows from *minimality* that there is some β such that $\alpha \leq \beta$ does not hold. Thus, by *connectivity* (Observation 2.48), $\beta < \alpha$, so that $\alpha \in \{\delta \mid \beta < \delta \text{ for some } \beta\}$.

For the other direction, let $\alpha \notin A$. It follows from *minimality* that $\alpha \leq \beta$ for all β, thus there is no β such that $\beta < \alpha$, thus $\alpha \notin \{\delta \mid \beta < \delta \text{ for some } \beta\}$.

135. $\alpha < \beta$ iff $\alpha \leq \beta$ and not $\beta \leq \alpha$
iff ($\alpha \notin A \div (\alpha \& \beta)$ or $\vdash \alpha \& \beta$) and not ($\beta \notin A \div (\alpha \& \beta)$ or $\vdash \alpha \& \beta$)
iff ($\alpha \notin A \div (\alpha \& \beta)$ or $\vdash \alpha \& \beta$) and $\beta \in A \div (\alpha \& \beta)$ and $\nvdash \alpha \& \beta$
iff $\alpha \notin A \div (\alpha \& \beta)$ and $\beta \in A \div (\alpha \& \beta)$ and $\nvdash \alpha \& \beta$
It follows by *closure* from $\alpha \notin A \div (\alpha \& \beta)$ that $\nvdash \alpha$ and consequently $\nvdash \alpha \& \beta$. We can continue:
iff $\alpha \notin A \div (\alpha \& \beta)$ and $\beta \in A \div (\alpha \& \beta)$

136. *Success*: Let $\nvdash\alpha$. We need to show that $\alpha \notin A+\alpha$. It follows by *dominance* that $\neg(\alpha<\alpha)$. It follows from this and $\nvdash\alpha$, by (R+), that $\alpha \notin A+\alpha$.

Extensionality: Let $\alpha\leftrightarrow\beta \in \mathrm{Cn}(\varnothing)$. We are first going to show that $A+\alpha \subseteq A+\beta$.

Let $\delta \in A+\alpha$. Then, by (R+), $\delta \in A$ and either $\alpha<\delta$ or $\vdash \alpha$. According to *intersubstitutivity* (Observation 2.92), $\alpha<\delta$ holds if and only if $\beta<\delta$.

We have shown that $\delta \in A$ and that either $\beta<\delta$ or $\vdash \alpha$. Again using (R+), we can conclude that $\delta \in A+\beta$.

Thus, $A+\alpha \subseteq A+\beta$. We can prove $A+\beta \subseteq A+\alpha$ in the same way, and conclude that $A+\alpha = A+\beta$.

Conjunctive overlap: Let $\delta \in (A+\alpha)\cap(A+\beta)$. There are two cases:

Case 1, $\vdash\alpha$: Then $\beta\leftrightarrow\alpha\&\beta \in \mathrm{Cn}(\varnothing)$. It follows by *extensionality*, that we have already proved, that $A+(\alpha\&\beta) = A+\beta$, and thus $\delta \in A+(\alpha\&\beta)$, as desired.

Case 2, $\nvdash\alpha$: It follows from *dominance* that $\alpha\&\beta\leq\alpha$. Furthermore, it follows from $\delta \in A+\alpha$ that $\alpha<\delta$. We can conclude, using *transitivity* and Observation 2.75, that $\alpha\&\beta<\delta$.

It follows by (R+) from $\delta \in A+\alpha$ that $\delta \in A$. We can conclude from $\delta \in A$ and $\alpha\&\beta<\delta$ that $\delta \in A+(\alpha\&\beta)$.

Conjunctive inclusion: Let $\alpha \notin A+(\alpha\&\beta)$. We have to show that $A+(\alpha\&\beta) \subseteq A+\alpha$.

Let $\delta \notin A+\alpha$. We are going to show that $\delta \notin A+(\alpha\&\beta)$. This follows by *inclusion* if $\delta \notin A$, so we may assume that $\delta \in A$.

Using (R+), we can conclude from $\delta \notin A+\alpha$ and $\delta \in A$ that $\neg(\alpha<\delta)$ and $\alpha \notin \mathrm{Cn}(\varnothing)$. By *connectivity* (Observation 2.48), $\delta\leq\alpha$.

Since $\alpha \notin A+(\alpha\&\beta)$ and $\alpha \in A$ it follows from (R+) that $\neg(\alpha\&\beta<\alpha)$. *Connectivity* yields $\alpha\leq\alpha\&\beta$.

We can now apply *transitivity* to $\delta\leq\alpha$ and $\alpha\leq\alpha\&\beta$ and obtain $\delta\leq\alpha\&\beta$, and thus $\neg(\alpha\&\beta<\delta)$. Since it follows from $\nvdash\alpha$ that $\nvdash\alpha\&\beta$, we can use (R+) to conclude that $\delta \notin A+(\alpha\&\beta)$, as desired.

137. a. Let $E(+) = \leq$ and $C(E(+)) = +'$. It follows from Part 1 of Theorem 2.50 that + is a standard entrenchment ordering and from Part 2 of the same Theorem that +' satisfies the eight postulates. We have:

$\beta \in A+'\alpha$ iff $\beta \in A$ and either $\vdash\alpha$ or $\alpha<\alpha\vee\beta$
iff $\beta \in A$ and either $\vdash\alpha$ or $((\alpha \notin A+\alpha)\&(\alpha\vee\beta \in A+\alpha))$ (Exercise 135)
iff $\beta \in A$ and either $\vdash\alpha$ or $\alpha\vee\beta \in A+\alpha$ (*success*)
iff $\beta \in A$ and either $\vdash\alpha$ or $\beta \in A+\alpha$ (Exercise 65)
iff $\beta \in A+\alpha$

b. Let $C(\leq) = +$ and $E(C\leq)) = \leq'$.
$\alpha\leq'\beta$ iff $\vdash\alpha\&\beta$ or $\alpha \notin A+(\alpha\&\beta)$
iff $\vdash\alpha\&\beta$ or not ($\alpha \in A$ and either $(\alpha\&\beta)<((\alpha\&\beta)\vee\alpha)$ or $\vdash(\alpha\&\beta)$)

iff $\vdash \alpha\&\beta$ or $\alpha \notin A$ or (not $(\alpha\&\beta)<((\alpha\&\beta)\vee\alpha)$ and $\nvdash(\alpha\&\beta)$)
iff $\vdash \alpha\&\beta$ or $\alpha \notin A$ or ($\alpha\leq(\alpha\&\beta)$ and $\nvdash(\alpha\&\beta)$)
iff $\vdash \alpha\&\beta$ or $\alpha \notin A$ or ($\alpha\leq\beta$ and $\nvdash(\alpha\&\beta)$) (Exercise 128, Part *c*)
(Due to *dominance*, $\vdash\alpha\&\beta$ implies $\alpha\leq\beta$. Due to *minimality*, $\alpha \notin A$ implies $\alpha\leq\beta$. Hence:)
iff $\alpha\leq\beta$

138. a. $\min(N(\alpha),N(\neg\alpha)) = N(\alpha\&\neg\alpha)$ (N2)
$= N(\perp)$ (N3)
$= 0$ (N1)
b. $N(\alpha\vee\beta) \geq \min(N(\alpha\vee\beta),N(\alpha\vee\neg\beta))$
$= N((\alpha\vee\beta)\&(\alpha\vee\neg\beta))$ (N2)
$= N(\alpha)$ (N3)
In the same way, we can obtain $N(\alpha\vee\beta) \geq N(\alpha)$. Since $\max(N(\alpha),N(\beta))$ is either $N(\alpha)$ or $N(\beta)$, it follows that $N(\alpha\vee\beta) \geq \max(N(\alpha),N(\beta))$.
c. Let $\alpha\vdash\beta$. Then:
$N(\alpha) = N(\alpha\&\beta)$ (N3)
$\leq \max(N(\alpha\&\beta),N(\neg\alpha\&\beta))$
$\leq N((\alpha\&\beta)\vee(\neg\alpha\&\beta))$ (Part *b* of this Exercise)
$= N(\beta)$ (N3)
d. Let $\beta \in \text{Cn}(\{\alpha \mid N(\alpha)>0\})$. Then, due to compactness, there is some finite subset A of $\{\alpha \mid N(\alpha)>0\}$ such that $\beta \in \text{Cn}(A)$ and consequently $\beta \in \text{Cn}(\{\&A\})$. It follows from repeated use of (N2) that $N(\&A)>0$. We can use Part *c* of the present exercise to obtain $N(\beta)\geq N(\&A)$, and hence $N(\beta)>0$.
e. *Transitivity*: Immediate.
Dominance: See Part *c* of the present exercise.
Conjunctiveness: Immediate from (N2).
Minimality:
$\alpha \notin \{\alpha \mid N(\alpha)>0\}$ iff $N(\alpha)=0$
iff $N(\alpha)\leq N(\beta)$ for all β
iff $\alpha\leq\beta$ for all β

SOLUTIONS FOR CHAPTER 3$^+$

139. a. $A \ddagger_\gamma \neg q$
$= \cap\gamma(A\perp q)\cup\{\neg q\}$
$= \cap\gamma(\{\{p\},\{p\rightarrow q\}\})\cup\{\neg q\}$
$= \cap(\{\{p\},\{p\rightarrow q\}\})\cup\{\neg q\}$
$= (\{p\}\cap\{p\rightarrow q\})\cup\{\neg q\}$
$= \{\neg q\}$.
b. $A \ddagger_\gamma(\neg p \vee \neg q)$
$= \cap\gamma(A\perp(p\&q))\cup\{\neg p\vee\neg q\}$
$= \cap\gamma(\{\{p\},\{p\rightarrow q,q\}\})\cup\{\neg p\vee\neg q\}$
$= \cap(\{\{p\rightarrow q,q\}\})\cup\{\neg p\vee\neg q\}$
$= \{p\rightarrow q,q\}\cup\{\neg p\vee\neg q\}$
$= \{p\rightarrow q,q,\neg p\vee\neg q\}$.
c. $A \ddagger_\gamma(\neg p \& \neg q)$
$= \cap\gamma(A\perp(p\vee q))\cup\{\neg p\&\neg q\}$
$= \cap\gamma(\{\{p\rightarrow q\}\})\cup\{\neg p\&\neg q\}$
$= \cap(\{\{p\rightarrow q\}\})\cup\{\neg p\&\neg q\}$
$= \{p\rightarrow q\}\cup\{\neg p\&\neg q\}$
$= \{p\rightarrow q,\neg p\&\neg q\}$.
d. $A \ddagger_\gamma(q\rightarrow p)$
$= \cap\gamma(A\perp(q\&\neg p))\cup\{q\rightarrow p\}$
$= \cap\gamma(\{A\})\cup\{q\rightarrow p\}$
$= \{A\}\cup\{q\rightarrow p\}$
$= \{p,p\rightarrow q,q\}\cup\{q\rightarrow p\}$
$= \{p,p\rightarrow q,q,q\rightarrow p\}$.

140. There are four subsets of A, namely A itself, $\varnothing$, $\{\neg p\}$ and $\{q\}$. Two of these, namely $\varnothing$ and $\{q\}$, retain consistency if p is added, and the same two retain consistency if $p\&r$ is added. It therefore follows from *uniformity* (that holds according to Theorem 3.6) that $A\cap(A\ddagger_\gamma p) = A\cap(A\ddagger_\gamma(p\&r))$.

141. a. Suppose that α is consistent. Then $\neg\alpha$ is not a tautology, and it follows (from the postulate of *contraction–success*) that $\neg\alpha \notin \mathrm{Cn}(A\sim_\gamma\neg\alpha)$. Since $\alpha\rightarrow\neg\alpha$ is logically equivalent with $\neg\alpha$, we have $\alpha\rightarrow\neg\alpha \notin \mathrm{Cn}(A\sim_\gamma\neg\alpha)$. It follows by the deduction property that $\neg\alpha \notin \mathrm{Cn}((A\sim_\gamma\neg\alpha)\cup\{\alpha\})$, i.e., $\neg\alpha \notin A\ddagger_\gamma\alpha$.
b. It follows from $A\sim_\gamma\neg\alpha \subseteq A$ that $(A\sim_\gamma\neg\alpha)\cup\{\alpha\} \subseteq A\cup\{\alpha\}$, i.e., $A\ddagger_\gamma\alpha \subseteq A\cup\{\alpha\}$.
c. $\alpha \in (A\sim_\gamma\neg\alpha)\cup\{\alpha\} = A\ddagger_\gamma\alpha$ follows directly from the definition.

d. Suppose that it holds for all $A' \subseteq A$ that $A' \cup \{\alpha\}$ is inconsistent if and only if $A' \cup \{\beta\}$ is inconsistent. $A' \cup \{\alpha\}$ is inconsistent if and only if $A' \vdash \neg\alpha$. Similarly, $A' \cup \{\beta\}$ is inconsistent if and only if $A' \vdash \neg\beta$. It therefore holds for all $A' \subseteq A$ that $A' \vdash \neg\alpha$ if and only if $A' \vdash \neg\beta$. It follows from Observation 1.39 that $A \perp \neg\alpha = A \perp \neg\beta$. From this we can conclude that $\cap\gamma(A \perp \neg\alpha) = \cap\gamma(A \perp \neg\beta)$, i.e., $A \sim_{\gamma} \neg\alpha = A \sim_{\gamma} \neg\beta$. By the Harper identity (Observation 3.11), this is equivalent to $A \cap (A \ddagger_{\gamma} \alpha) = A \cap (A \ddagger_{\gamma} \beta)$.

142. No. Internal partial meet revision satisfies *consistency*. It follows from *consistency* that if α is consistent and A is inconsistent, then $A * \alpha$ is consistent, and thus $A * \alpha \neq A$.

143. We will do this by showing that $A * \alpha * \neg\alpha \neq A * \neg\alpha * \alpha$, where α is a sentence such that neither α nor $\neg\alpha$ is inconsistent. It follows from *success* that $\neg\alpha \in A * \alpha * \neg\alpha$, and then from *consistency* that $\alpha \notin A * \alpha * \neg\alpha$. It follows from *success* that $\alpha \in A * \neg\alpha * \alpha$.

144. a. $\{p,q\} \ddagger \neg p$
$= \cap(\{p,q\} \perp p) \cup \{\neg p\}$
$= \cap\{\{q\}\} \cup \{\neg p\}$
$= \{q\} \cup \{\neg p\}$
$= \{\neg p, q\}$
b. $\{p,q\} \ddagger (\neg p \vee \neg q)$
$= \cap(\{p,q\} \perp (p \& q)) \cup \{\neg p \vee \neg q\}$
$= \cap\{\{p\},\{q\}\} \cup \{\neg p \vee \neg q\}$
$= \varnothing \cup \{\neg p \vee \neg q\}$
$= \{\neg p \vee \neg q\}$
c. $\{p,q,p \rightarrow q\} \ddagger (p \& \neg q)$
$= \cap(\{p,q,p \rightarrow q\} \perp (\neg p \vee q)) \cup \{p \& \neg q\}$
$= \cap\{\{p\}\} \cup \{p \& \neg q\}$
$= \{p\} \cup \{p \& \neg q\}$
$= \{p, p \& \neg q\}$
d. $\{p \rightarrow q, q \rightarrow p\} \ddagger (p \leftrightarrow \neg q)$
$= \cap(\{p \rightarrow q, q \rightarrow p\} \perp (p \leftrightarrow q)) \cup \{p \leftrightarrow \neg q\}$
$= \cap\{\{p \rightarrow q\},\{q \rightarrow p\}\} \cup \{p \leftrightarrow \neg q\}$
$= \varnothing \cup \{p \leftrightarrow \neg q\}$
$= \{p \leftrightarrow \neg q\}$.

145. Let $*$ be internal full meet revision. Then $\{p,q\} * (\neg p \vee \neg q) = \{\neg p \vee \neg q\}$. Thus, *tenacity* is not satisfied. (To see this, note that $p \in \{p,q\}$, $p \notin \{\neg p \vee \neg q\}$ and $\neg p \notin \text{Cn}(\{\neg p \vee \neg q\})$.) It follows from Theorem 3.33 that $*$ is not internal maxichoice revision.

146. *Case 1*, α is consistent: Then $\neg\alpha$ is not a tautology, and thus $A\bot\neg\alpha$ is non-empty. It follows that $\varnothing \neq \gamma(A\bot\neg\alpha) \subseteq A\bot\neg\alpha$, and thus $\cap(A\bot\neg\alpha) \subseteq \cap\gamma(A\bot\neg\alpha)$. We can conclude that $(\cap(A\bot\neg\alpha))\cup\{\alpha\} \subseteq (\cap\gamma(A\bot\neg\alpha))\cup\{\alpha\}$, i.e., $A\ddagger\alpha \subseteq A\ddagger_\gamma\alpha$.

Case 2, α is inconsistent: Then $\neg\alpha$ is a tautology, and thus $A\bot\neg\alpha$ is empty. It follows that $A\sim\neg\alpha = A\sim_\gamma\neg\alpha = A$, and thus $(A\sim\neg\alpha)\cup\{\alpha\} = (A\sim_\gamma\neg\alpha)\cup\{\alpha\}$, i.e., $A\ddagger\alpha = A\ddagger_\gamma\alpha$.

147. *For one direction*, let $\varepsilon \in A+\alpha\ddagger\alpha$. Suppose that $\varepsilon \notin A\ddagger\alpha$. Then ε is not identical to α, and we can conclude from $\varepsilon \in A+\alpha\ddagger\alpha$ that $\varepsilon \in A$. It follows from $\varepsilon \notin A\ddagger\alpha$ that $\varepsilon \notin A\sim\neg\alpha$, i.e., $\varepsilon \notin \cap(A\bot\neg\alpha)$. There must be some X such that $\varepsilon \notin X \in A\bot\neg\alpha$.

We can use Observation 1.41 to obtain $X\cup\{\alpha\} \in (A\cup\{\alpha\})\bot\neg\alpha$. Since ε is not identical to α, and $\varepsilon \notin X$, we have $\varepsilon \notin X\cup\{\alpha\} \in (A\cup\{\alpha\})\bot\neg\alpha$, from which follows that $\varepsilon \notin \cap((A\cup\{\alpha\})\bot\neg\alpha)$, i.e., $\varepsilon \notin \cap((A+\alpha)\bot\neg\alpha)$. Again using the fact that ε is not identical to α, we obtain $\varepsilon \notin (\cap((A+\alpha)\bot\neg\alpha))\cup\{\alpha\}$, i.e., $\varepsilon \notin A+\alpha\ddagger\alpha$. We can conclude from this contradiction that $\varepsilon \in A\ddagger\alpha$. This finishes our proof that $A+\alpha\ddagger\alpha \subseteq A\ddagger\alpha$.

For the other direction, let $\varepsilon \in A\ddagger\alpha$. We are going to show that $\varepsilon \in A+\alpha\ddagger\alpha$. This follows directly if ε is identical to α. It remains to prove the principal case in which $\varepsilon \in (A\ddagger\alpha)\setminus\{\alpha\}$. It follows from $\varepsilon \in (A\ddagger\alpha)\setminus\{\alpha\}$ that $\varepsilon \in \cap(A\bot\neg\alpha)$.

Let $X \in (A\cup\{\alpha\})\bot\neg\alpha$. If $\alpha \in A$, then $X \in A\bot\neg\alpha$, and it follows directly from $\varepsilon \in \cap(A\bot\neg\alpha)$ that $\varepsilon \in X$. If $\alpha \notin A$, then it follows from Observation 1.41 that $X\setminus\{\alpha\} \in A\bot\neg\alpha$, so that we can conclude from $\varepsilon \in \cap(A\bot\neg\alpha)$ that $\varepsilon \in X\setminus\{\alpha\}$ and consequently $\varepsilon \in X$. Thus in both cases, $\varepsilon \in X$.

Since $\varepsilon \in X$ for all $X \in (A\cup\{\alpha\})\bot\neg\alpha$, we have $\varepsilon \in \cap((A\cup\{\alpha\})\bot\neg\alpha)$ and consequently $\varepsilon \in (\cap((A\cup\{\alpha\})\bot\neg\alpha))\cup\{\alpha\}$, i.e., $\varepsilon \in A+\alpha\ddagger\alpha$. This concludes the proof that $A\ddagger\alpha \subseteq A+\alpha\ddagger\alpha$.

148. Let p and q be two logically independent sentences of the language, and let $A = \{\neg p\&q\}$. Then $A\bot\neg p = \{\varnothing\}$, and consequently it holds for all selection functions γ for A that $A\sim_\gamma\neg p = \varnothing$, and thus $A\ddagger_\gamma p = \{p\}$.We then have $q \in \mathrm{Cn}(A)$, but neither $q \in \mathrm{Cn}(A\ddagger_\gamma p)$ nor $\neg q \in \mathrm{Cn}(A\ddagger_\gamma p)$.

149. a. $\{p,q\rightarrow p\}\pm_\gamma\neg p$
$= \cap\gamma(\{p,q\rightarrow p,\neg p\}\bot p)$
$= \cap\gamma\{\{q\rightarrow p,\neg p\}\}$
$= \cap\{\{q\rightarrow p,\neg p\}\}$
$= \{q\rightarrow p,\neg p\}$.
b. $\{p,q\rightarrow r,\neg q\rightarrow r\}\pm_\gamma(\neg p\vee\neg r)$

$= \cap\gamma(\{p, q\rightarrow r, \neg q\rightarrow r, \neg p\vee\neg r\}\perp(p\&r))$
$= \cap\gamma(\{\{p, \neg q\rightarrow r, \neg p\vee\neg r\}, \{p, q\rightarrow r, \neg p\vee\neg r\}, \{q\rightarrow r, \neg q\rightarrow r, \neg p\vee\neg r\}\}$
$= \cap\{\{p, \neg q\rightarrow r, \neg p\vee\neg r\}, \{p, q\rightarrow r, \neg p\vee\neg r\}, \{q\rightarrow r, \neg q\rightarrow r, \neg p\vee\neg r\}\} =$
$= \{\neg p\vee\neg r\}$

c. $\{p, q, q\&r\}\pm_\gamma(p\&q)$
$= \cap\gamma(\{p, q, q\&r, p\&q\}\perp(\neg p\vee\neg q))$
$= \cap\gamma(\{\{p, q, q\&r, p\&q\}\})$
$= \cap\{\{p, q, q\&r, p\&q\}\}$
$= \{p, q, q\&r, p\&q\}$

d. $\{p, q, q\&r\}\pm_\gamma\neg(p\&q)$
$= \cap\gamma(\{p, q, q\&r, \neg(p\&q)\})\perp(p\&q))$
$= \cap\gamma(\{\{p, \neg(p\&q)\}, \{q, q\&r, \neg(p\&q)\}\})$
$= \cap(\{\{q, q\&r, \neg(p\&q)\}\})$
$= \{q, q\&r, \neg(p\&q)\}$

150. *Consistency*: If α is consistent, then $\neg\alpha$ is not a tautology, and thus (by *contraction-success*) $(A+\alpha)\sim_\gamma\neg\alpha \nvdash \neg\alpha$, i.e., $A\pm_\gamma\alpha \nvdash \neg\alpha$.

Inclusion: It follows from *contraction-inclusion* that $(A+\alpha)\sim_\gamma\neg\alpha \subseteq A+\alpha$, i.e., $A\pm_\gamma\alpha \subseteq A+\alpha$.

Success: Suppose to the contrary that $\alpha \notin A\pm_\gamma\alpha$, i.e., $\alpha \notin (A+\alpha)\sim_\gamma\neg\alpha$ There is then some $X \in \gamma((A+\alpha)\perp\neg\alpha)$ such that $\alpha \notin X$. This is impossible according to Observation 3.30.

Pre-expansion: It follows from $A\cup\{\alpha\}\cup\{\alpha\} = A\cup\{\alpha\}$ that $(A\cup\{\alpha\}\cup\{\alpha\})\sim_\gamma\neg\alpha = (A\cup\{\alpha\})\sim_\gamma\neg\alpha$, i.e.,
$((A+\alpha)+\alpha)\sim_\gamma\neg\alpha = (A+\alpha)\sim_\gamma\neg\alpha$, i.e.,
$(A+\alpha)\pm_\gamma\alpha = A\pm_\gamma\alpha$.

151. If $\alpha \in A$, then it follows from Observation 3.30 that $\alpha \in A\sim_\gamma\neg\alpha$. Therefore, $A\pm_\gamma\alpha = (A\cup\{\alpha\})\sim_\gamma\neg\alpha = A\sim_\gamma\neg\alpha = (A\sim_\gamma\neg\alpha)\cup\{\alpha\} = A\mp_\gamma\alpha$.

152. Let $A\perp\neg\alpha = \{X\}$. It follows that $A\sim_\gamma\neg\alpha = X$ and consequently $A\mp_\gamma\alpha = X\cup\{\alpha\}$.

It follows from Observation 1.41 that $\{X\cup\{\alpha\}\} = (A\cup\{\alpha\})\perp\neg\alpha$, and consequently $A\pm_\gamma\alpha = X\cup\{\alpha\}$.

153. Let p and q be logically independent sentences, and let γ be a maxichoice selection function such that:
$\gamma(\{\{p\vee q, \neg p\}, \{p\vee\neg q, \neg p\}\}) = \{\{p\vee q, \neg p\}\}$
$\gamma(\{\{p\vee q, \neg p\&\neg r\}, \{p\vee\neg q, \neg p\&\neg r\}\}) = \{\{p\vee\neg q, \neg p\&\neg r\}\}$
Then:
$\{p\vee q, p\vee\neg q\}\pm_\gamma\neg p = \{p\vee q, \neg p\}$
$\{p\vee q, p\vee\neg q\}\pm_\gamma(\neg p\&\neg r) = \{p\vee\neg q, \neg p\&\neg r\}$

Since every subset of $\{p\vee q, p\vee\neg q\}$ is inconsistent with $\neg p$ if and only if it is inconsistent with $\neg p\&\neg r$, this shows that uniformity is not sâtisfied.

154. Let $A = \{\neg p\vee r, \neg p\vee\neg r\}$ and let γ be a two-place selection function that is based on a relation $\sqsubseteq$ such that:
$\{\neg p\vee r\} \sqsubset \{\neg p\vee\neg r\} \sqsubset \{p,\neg p\vee\neg r\} \sqsubset \{p,\neg p\vee r\}$.
This is compatible with γ being maxichoice and with $\sqsubseteq$ being maximizing and transitive. Then:

$A\mp_\gamma p = (\cap\gamma(A\perp\neg p))\cup\{p\}$
$= (\cap\gamma(\{\{\neg p\vee r\},\{\neg p\vee\neg r\}\}))\cup\{p\}$
$= \{\neg p\vee\neg r\}\cup\{p\}$
$= \{\neg p\vee\neg r, p\}$

and:

$A\pm_\gamma p = \cap\gamma((A\cup\{p\})\perp\neg p)$
$= \cap\gamma(\{\{p,\neg p\vee\neg r\},\{p,\neg p\vee r\}\})$
$= \{p,\neg p\vee r\}$

It follows that $A\mp_\gamma p \not\subseteq A\pm_\gamma p$ and $A\pm_\gamma p \not\subseteq A\mp_\gamma p$

155. a. $\{\perp,\neg\alpha\}$
b. $\neg\alpha$
c. $\{\perp,\neg\alpha,\neg\beta,\neg\delta,\neg\alpha\vee\neg\beta,\neg\alpha\vee\neg\delta,\neg\beta\vee\neg\delta,\neg\alpha\vee\neg\beta\vee\neg\delta\}\}$
d. $\neg\alpha\vee\neg\beta\vee\neg\delta$

156. a. $X = \{\neg p,\neg q\}$
b. $X = \{\neg p\&\neg q\}$
c. This equation has no solution, since for all X, if $p, q \in \neg X$, then $p\vee q \in \neg X$.

157. Let $\varepsilon \in B\cap\neg B$: There are, according to Definition 3.35, three cases:
(1) ε is inconsistent. Then we are done.
(2) ε is equivalent to $\neg\delta$ for some $\delta \in B$: Then $\{\varepsilon,\delta\} \subseteq B$, and B is inconsistent.
(3) ε is equivalent to $\neg\delta_1\vee\ldots\neg\delta_n$ for some $\delta_1,\ldots\delta_n \in B$. Then $\{\varepsilon,\delta_1,\ldots\delta_n\}$ is inconsistent, and since $\{\varepsilon,\delta_1,\ldots\delta_n\} \subseteq B$, so is B.

158. *For one direction*, let $B \vdash \perp$. Then by compactness there is a finite subset $\{\beta_1,\ldots\beta_n\}$ of B such that $\{\beta_1,\ldots\beta_n\} \vdash \perp$. We have:

$\{\beta_1,\ldots\beta_n\} \vdash \perp$
$\beta_1\&\ldots\beta_n \vdash \perp$
$\vdash \beta_1\&\ldots\beta_n \rightarrow \perp$ (deduction property)
$\vdash \neg(\beta_1\&\ldots\beta_n)$
$\vdash \neg\beta_1\vee\ldots\neg\beta_n$

$\neg\beta_1 \vee ... \neg\beta_n \in \mathrm{Cn}(\varnothing)$

By Definition 3.35, $\neg\beta_1 \vee ... \neg\beta_n \in \neg B$. We can conclude that $\neg B \cap \mathrm{Cn}(\varnothing) \neq \varnothing$.

For the other direction, let $\neg B \cap \mathrm{Cn}(\varnothing) \neq \varnothing$. Then there is a finite subset $\{\beta_1,...\beta_n\}$ of B sucht that $\neg\beta_1 \vee ... \neg\beta_n \in \mathrm{Cn}(\varnothing)$, i.e., $\vdash \neg\beta_1 \vee ... \neg\beta_n$, i.e., $\vdash \neg(\beta_1 \& ... \& \beta_n)$, i.e., $\vdash \beta_1 \& ... \& \beta_n \rightarrow \perp$, i.e., $\beta_1 \& ... \& \beta \vdash \perp$. Hence, $B \vdash \perp$.

159. a. Suppose to the contrary that $\beta \in A \cap B$ and $\beta \notin X \in A \perp \neg B$. It follows from $\beta \in A \setminus X$ and $X \in A \perp \neg B$ that there is some sentence $\delta \in \neg B$ such that $X \cup \{\beta\} \vdash \delta$. By the deduction property, $X \vdash \beta \rightarrow \delta$, or equivalently $X \vdash \neg\beta \vee \delta$.

It follows from $\beta \in B$ and $\delta \in \neg B$, by the construction of $\neg B$, that $\neg\beta \vee \delta \in \neg B$. It follows from this and $X \vdash \neg\beta \vee \delta$ that $X \notin A \perp \neg B$, contrary to the conditions. This contradiction concludes the proof.

b. Directly from Part *a* since if $B \subseteq A$, then $A \cap B = B$.

160. *For one direction*, let $X \in (A \cup B) \perp \neg B$. It follows from Exercise 159 that $B \subseteq X$. To prove that $X \in (A \cup B) \perp \perp$, suppose to the contrary that this is not so. Since X is a subset of $A \cup B$ that does not imply $\perp$ (note that $\perp \in \neg B$), there must then be some $\varepsilon \in (A \cup B) \setminus X$ such that $X \cup \{\varepsilon\} \nvdash \perp$. However, it follows from $X \in (A \cup B) \perp \neg B$ that ε implies some element of $\neg B$. Since $B \subseteq X$ and every element of $\neg B$ is inconsistent with B (i.e., if $\zeta \in \neg B$, then $B \cup \{\zeta\}$ is inconsistent), we can conclude that $X \cup \{\varepsilon\} \vdash \perp$. This contradiction is sufficient to establish that $X \in (A \cup B) \perp \perp$.

For the other direction, let $B \subseteq X \in (A \cup B) \perp \perp$. Then (again since every element if $\neg B$ is inconsistent with B) $(\neg B) \cap \mathrm{Cn}(X) = \varnothing$. Suppose that $X \notin (A \cup B) \perp \neg B$. Since X is a subset of $A \cup B$ that does not imply any element of $\neg B$ there must then be some $\varepsilon \in (A \cup B) \setminus X$ such that $(\neg B) \cap \mathrm{Cn}(X \cup \{\varepsilon\}) = \varnothing$. Since $\neg B$ is non-empty, it follows from this that $X \cup \{\varepsilon\}$ is consistent, contrary to $X \in (A \cup B) \perp \perp$. This contradiction concludes the proof.

161. a. Let $B \subseteq A$. It follows from Exercise 159b that if $X \in A \perp \neg B$, then $B \subseteq X$. From this we can conclude that $B \subseteq A \sim_\gamma \neg B$. Therefore: $A \pm_\gamma B = (A \cup B) \sim_\gamma \neg B = A \sim_\gamma \neg B = (A \sim_\gamma \neg B) \cup B = A \mp_\gamma B$.

b. Let B be inconsistent. It follows from Exercise 158 that $\neg B$ contains a tautology, and thus $A \sim_\gamma \neg B = A$, and consequently $A \mp_\gamma B = A \cup B$.

162. a. Let B be consistent. It follows from Exercise 158 that $\neg B \cap \mathrm{Cn}(\varnothing) = \varnothing$. It follows (by the contraction-postulate of *P-success*) that $\neg B \cap \mathrm{Cn}(A \sim_\gamma \neg B) = \varnothing$, and consequently that $A \mp_\gamma B = (A \sim_\gamma \neg B) \cup \{\varepsilon\}$ is consistent.

b. There are two cases, depending on whether or not B is consistent.

If B is inconsistent, then if follows from Exercise 158 that $\neg B \cap \mathrm{Cn}(\varnothing) \neq \varnothing$. Then $A \perp \neg B$ is empty so that $\gamma(A \perp \neg B) = \{A\}$ and consequently $A \ddagger_\gamma \alpha = \cap\gamma(A \perp \neg B) \cup B = A \cup B$. Thus, there can be no ε such that $\varepsilon \in A$ and $\varepsilon \notin A \ddagger_\gamma B$, and *relevance* is vacuously satisfied.

If B is consistent, let $\varepsilon \in A \setminus (A \ddagger_\gamma B)$. Then $\varepsilon \notin A \sim_\gamma \neg B$, so that there must be some X such that $\varepsilon \notin X \in \gamma(A \perp \neg B)$. It follows that $\neg B \cap \mathrm{Cn}(X) = \varnothing$ and $\neg B \cap \mathrm{Cn}(X \cup \{\varepsilon\}) \neq \mathrm{Cn}(\varnothing)$. It follows from this that $X \cup B$ is consistent and $(X \cup B) \cup \{\varepsilon\}$ is inconsistent. We can also conclude from the definition of internal partial meet revision that $A \ddagger_\gamma B \subseteq X \cup B \subseteq A \cup B$. Hence, *P-relevance* is satified.

163. a. Let $ML\alpha \in m(A_0)$. Then there is some A' such that $A_0 R A'$ and $L\alpha \in m(A')$. It follows that $\alpha \in m(A'+B+\perp)$ for all B.

Let A'' be any belief base such that $A_0 R A''$. Then we have $\alpha \in m(A'+A''+\perp) = m(A''+A'+\perp)$, so that $M\alpha \in m(A'')$. Since this holds for all A'' such that $A_0 R A''$, we may conclude that $LM\alpha \in m(A_0)$.

b–c. As in Observation 3.46.

d. It follows from Part *a* that $MLM\alpha \vDash LMM\alpha$. By $MM\alpha \vDash M\alpha$ (Part *c*) and (DR1) follows $LMM\alpha \vDash LM\alpha$. It follows that $MLM\alpha \vDash LM\alpha$. By Part 3 of Observation 3.44 follows $LM\alpha \vDash MLM\alpha$. We may conclude that $MLM\alpha \dashv\vDash LM\alpha$.

e. Apply Part 1 of Observation 3.44 to $MLM\alpha \dashv\vDash LM\alpha$ that was obtained in Part *d*.

f. In the same way as in Theorem 3.44, we can reduce any formula to either the form $\Pi B\alpha$ or the form $\neg\Pi B\alpha$, where Π is a (possibly empty) sequence of L and M. Using parts b-c of the present exercise we can delete any repetitions of L or M in Π. After that, parts d and e of the present exercise can be used to shorten any sequence of three or more letters L and M. What remains are formulas of the ten mentioned forms.

g. $LB\alpha \vDash MLB\alpha$: From Part 3 of Observation 3.44.
$MLB\alpha \vDash LMB\alpha$: From Part *a* of this exercise.
$LMB\alpha \vDash MB\alpha$: From Part 2 of Observation 3.44.
$LB\alpha \vDash B\alpha$: From Part 2 of Observation 3.44.
$B\alpha \vDash MB\alpha$: From Part 3 of Observation 3.44.

164. Suppose that *success* and *closure* are satisfied, and that $\alpha \vdash \beta$. It follows from *success* that $\alpha \in A*\alpha$, and then from $\alpha \vdash \beta$ that $\beta \in \mathrm{Cn}(A*\alpha)$. By *closure*, $\mathrm{Cn}(A*\alpha) = A*\alpha$, so that $\beta \in A*\alpha$.

165. a. *Vacuity.*

b. One direction: *Preservation* follows from *vacuity* alone.

The other direction: Let $\neg\alpha \notin \text{Cn}(A)$. It follows from *inclusion* that $A*\alpha \subseteq A+\alpha$. It follows from *success* that $\alpha \in A*\alpha$ and from *preservation* that $A \subseteq A*\alpha$; thus $A+\alpha = A*\alpha$, and we are done.

166. Suppose that $*$ satisfies *success, closure*, and *reciprocity*, and let $\alpha\leftrightarrow\beta \in \text{Cn}(\varnothing)$. It follows from *success* that $\alpha \in A*\alpha$. From this and $\alpha\leftrightarrow\beta \in \text{Cn}(\varnothing)$ we can conclude that $\beta \in \text{Cn}(A*\alpha)$. By *closure*, $\text{Cn}(A*\alpha) = A*\alpha$, so that $\beta \in A*\alpha$. It follows in exactly the same way that $\alpha \in A*\beta$, and we can apply *reciprocity* to conclude that $A*\alpha = A*\beta$.

167. There are two cases, according to whether or not $\alpha\vee\beta$ is consistent.

Case 1, $\alpha\vee\beta$ is inconsistent: Then α is inconsistent, and it follows from *success* that $A*\alpha$ is inconsistent, so that $\text{Cn}((A*\alpha)\cup(A*\beta)) = \mathcal{L}$, from which $A*(\alpha\vee\beta) \subseteq \text{Cn}((A*\alpha)\cup(A*\beta))$ follows directly.

Case 2, $\alpha\vee\beta$ is consistent: We are first going to show that either $\neg\alpha \notin A*(\alpha\vee\beta)$ or $\neg\beta \notin A*(\alpha\vee\beta)$. Suppose to the contrary that $\neg\alpha \in A*(\alpha\vee\beta)$ and $\neg\beta \in A*(\alpha\vee\beta)$. Then $\neg\alpha\&\neg\beta \in \text{Cn}(A*(\alpha\vee\beta))$. It follows from *success* that $\alpha\vee\beta \in A*(\alpha\vee\beta)$. Since $\neg\alpha\&\neg\beta$ and $\alpha\vee\beta$ together are inconsistent, it follows that $A*(\alpha\vee\beta)$ is inconsistent. Since in this case $\alpha\vee\beta$ is consistent, this contradicts the postulate of *consistency*. We can conclude from this contradiction that either $\neg\alpha \notin A*(\alpha\vee\beta)$ or $\neg\beta \notin A*(\alpha\vee\beta)$.

If $\neg\alpha \notin A*(\alpha\vee\beta)$, then it follows from *disjunctive inclusion* that $A*(\alpha\vee\beta) \subseteq A*\alpha$, and if $\neg\beta \notin A*(\alpha\vee\beta)$ that $A*(\alpha\vee\beta) \subseteq A*\beta$. In both cases, $A*(\alpha\vee\beta) \subseteq \text{Cn}((A*\alpha)\cup(A*\beta))$, which concludes the proof.

168. a. Let $A*\alpha = A*\beta$. It follows from *success* that $\alpha \in A*\alpha$. It also follows from *success* that $\beta \in A*\beta$, and thus $\beta \in A*\alpha$. Since α and β together imply $\alpha\leftrightarrow\beta$, we can conclude that $\alpha\leftrightarrow\beta \in \text{Cn}(A*\alpha)$, and *closure* yields $\alpha\leftrightarrow\beta \in A*\alpha$.

b. Let $A*\alpha = A*\beta$. We showed in Part *a* that $\alpha\leftrightarrow\beta \in A*\alpha$. By *inclusion*, $A*\alpha \subseteq \text{Cn}(A\cup\{\alpha\})$, and thus $\alpha\leftrightarrow\beta \in \text{Cn}(A\cup\{\alpha\})$. By the deduction property, $\alpha\rightarrow(\alpha\leftrightarrow\beta) \in \text{Cn}(A)$, or equivalently $\alpha\rightarrow\beta \in \text{Cn}(A)$.

It also follows from Part *a* that $\alpha\leftrightarrow\beta \in A*\beta$. By the same argument, we can conclude that $\beta\rightarrow\alpha \in \text{Cn}(A)$.

It follows from $\alpha\rightarrow\beta \in \text{Cn}(A)$ and $\beta\rightarrow\alpha \in \text{Cn}(A)$ that $\alpha\leftrightarrow\beta \in \text{Cn}(A)$, and since A is logically closed we can conclude that $\alpha\leftrightarrow\beta \in A$.

169. We use *inclusion* to obtain $A*\alpha \subseteq \text{Cn}(A\cup\{\alpha\})$ and then set theory to obtain $A*\alpha = (A*\alpha) \cap \text{Cn}(A\cup\{\alpha\})$. By *success* and *closure*, $A*\alpha = \text{Cn}((A*\alpha)\cup\{\alpha\})$. We therefore have:

$$A*\alpha = \text{Cn}((A*\alpha)\cup\{\alpha\}) \cap \text{Cn}(A\cup\{\alpha\})$$

The right-hand side of this expression can be simplified as follows:

$\beta \in \text{Cn}((A*\alpha)\cup\{\alpha\}) \cap \text{Cn}(A\cup\{\alpha\})$
iff $\beta \in \text{Cn}((A*\alpha)\cup\{\alpha\})$ and $\beta \in \text{Cn}(A\cup\{\alpha\})$
iff $\alpha\rightarrow\beta \in \text{Cn}(A*\alpha)$ and $\alpha\rightarrow\beta \in \text{Cn}(A)$ (deduction property)
(By *closure*, $\text{Cn}(A*\alpha) = A*\alpha$, and since A is logically closed $\text{Cn}(A) = A$. We can continue:)
iff $\alpha\rightarrow\beta \in A*\alpha$ and $\alpha\rightarrow\beta \in A$
iff $\alpha\rightarrow\beta \in A\cap(A*\alpha)$
iff $\beta \in \text{Cn}((A\cap(A*\alpha))\cup\{\alpha\})$ (deduction property)
iff $\beta \in (A\cap(A*\alpha))+\alpha$
Thus, $A*\alpha = \text{Cn}((A*\alpha)\cup\{\alpha\}) \cap \text{Cn}(A\cup\{\alpha\}) = (A\cap(A*\alpha))+\alpha$.

170. a. For one direction, let $\alpha \vdash \beta$. It follows from *inclusion* that $A_0*\beta \subseteq \text{Cn}(A_0\cup\{\beta\})$, i.e., $A_0*\beta \subseteq \text{Cn}(\{\beta\})$. Furthermore, it follows from *success* that $\alpha \in A_0*\alpha$, and since $\alpha \vdash \beta$ we can conclude that $\beta \in A_0*\alpha$ and thus $\text{Cn}(\{\beta\}) \subseteq \text{Cn}(A_0*\alpha)$. By *closure*, $\text{Cn}(A_0*\alpha) = A_0*\alpha$, and thus $A_0*\beta \subseteq \text{Cn}(\{\beta\}) \subseteq A_0*\alpha$.

For the other direction, let $A_0*\beta \subseteq A_0*\alpha$. It follows from *success* that $\beta \in A_0*\beta$ and from *inclusion* that $A_0*\alpha \subseteq \text{Cn}(A_0\cup\{\alpha\})$, i.e., $A_0*\alpha \subseteq \text{Cn}(\{\alpha\})$. We therefore have $\beta \in \text{Cn}(\{\alpha\})$, i.e., $\alpha \vdash \beta$.

b. Let p and q be logically independent sentences such that $p\&q$ is consistent. Let $A = \text{Cn}(\{p,\neg q\})$. Without violating the three postulates we may let $A*p = A$. It follows that $\neg q \in A*p$.

It follows from *success* that $p\&q \in A*(p\&q)$, and from *consistency* that $A*(p\&q)$ is consistent. We can conclude from this that $\neg q \notin A*(p\&q)$, and thus $A*p \not\subseteq A*(p\&q)$. Since $\vdash p\&q \rightarrow p$, this is sufficient for the desired negative result.

171. *Case 1*, α is inconsistent: It follows from *success* that both $A*\alpha$ and $(A*\alpha)*\alpha$ are inconsistent, and from *closure* that they are both logically closed. They are therefore both identical to $\mathcal{L}$, so that $A*\alpha = (A*\alpha)*\alpha$.

Case 2, α is consistent: It follows from *success* that $\alpha \in A*\alpha$, and then from *consistency* that $\neg\alpha \notin A*\alpha$ and from *vacuity* that $(A*\alpha)*\alpha = \text{Cn}((A*\alpha)\cup\{\alpha\})$. Due to *success* and *closure*, $\text{Cn}((A*\alpha)\cup\{\alpha\}) = A*\alpha$, and we may conclude that $(A*\alpha)*\alpha = A*\alpha$.

172. a. This can be proved in the same way as Exercise 143.
b. Let p and q be logically independent sentences, and let A be an arbitrary belief set. Suppose that *vacuity*, *consistency*, and *monotonicity* all hold.

It follows from *vacuity* that $\text{Cn}(\{p\})*(\neg p\vee\neg q) = \text{Cn}(\{p,\neg p\vee\neg q\})$ and from *monotonicity* that $\{p,\neg p\vee\neg q\} \subseteq \text{Cn}(\{p,q\})*(\neg p\vee\neg q)$.

In the same way we can show that $\{q,\neg p\vee\neg q\} \subseteq \text{Cn}(\{p,q\})*(\neg p\vee\neg q)$.

It follows from $\{p,\neg p\vee\neg q\} \subseteq \mathrm{Cn}(\{p,q\})*(\neg p\vee\neg q)$ and $\{q,\neg p\vee\neg q\} \subseteq \mathrm{Cn}(\{p,q\})*(\neg p\vee\neg q)$ that $\{p,q,\neg p\vee\neg q\} \subseteq \mathrm{Cn}(\{p,q\})*(\neg p\vee\neg q)$, contrary to *consistency*. This contradiction concludes the proof.

c. Let $A_1 \subseteq A_2$. Then we have:
$A_1*\alpha = (A_1\cap A_2)*\alpha$
$= A_1*\alpha \cap A_2*\alpha$
$\subseteq A_2*\alpha$
so that *monotonicity* holds, which we have shown in Part *b* to be impossible.

d. Suppose to the contrary that the four postulates all hold. Let p and q be logically independent sentences. (Remember that $\top$ denotes a tautology and $\perp$ a contradiction.) We then have:
$\mathrm{Cn}(\{p\}) = \mathrm{Cn}(\{p\})*\top$ (*vacuity*)
$= \mathrm{Cn}(\{p\})*\perp*\top$ (the new postulate)
$= \mathcal{L}*\top$ (*success* and *closure*)
$= \mathrm{Cn}(\{q\})*\perp*\top$ (*success* and *closure*)
$= \mathrm{Cn}(\{q\})*\top$ (the new postulate)
$= \mathrm{Cn}(\{q\})$ (*vacuity*)
so that p and q are logically equivalent, contrary to our conditions. This contradiction concludes the proof.

173. It follows from $\beta\rightarrow\alpha \in A+\alpha$ by *contraction-closure* that $\neg\alpha\rightarrow\neg\beta \in A+\alpha$. We have $A*\neg\alpha = \mathrm{Cn}((A+\neg\neg\alpha)\cup\{\neg\alpha\})$, which is by *contraction-extensionality* equivalent to $A*\neg\alpha = \mathrm{Cn}((A+\alpha)\cup\{\neg\alpha\})$. Since $\neg\alpha$ and $\neg\alpha\rightarrow\neg\beta$ together imply $\neg\beta$, we can conclude that $\neg\beta \in A*\neg\alpha$.

174. It follows from $+ = \mathbb{C}(*)$ that $A+\alpha = A\cap(A*\neg\alpha)$. It follows from the logical closure and inconsistency of A that $\neg\alpha \in A$ and from *revision-success* that $\neg\alpha \in A*\neg\alpha$, so that $\neg\alpha \in A\cap(A*\neg\alpha) = A+\alpha$ as desired.

175. a. We need to show that $\mathbb{R}(+') = \mathbb{R}(+)$, i.e., $\mathbb{R}(\mathbb{C}(\mathbb{R}(+))) = \mathbb{R}(+)$. It follows from Observation 3.54 that $\mathbb{R}(+)$ satisfies all the basic revision-postulates, and thus from Observation 3.57 that $\mathbb{R}(\mathbb{C}(\mathbb{R}(+))) = \mathbb{R}(+)$.

b. Let $\mathbb{R}(+) = *$. We then have $+' = \mathbb{C}(*)$. It follows that $A+'\alpha = A\cap(A*\neg\alpha)$. Using $* = \mathbb{R}(+)$ we obtain $A+'\alpha = A\cap\mathrm{Cn}((A+\neg\neg\alpha)\cup\{\neg\alpha\})$. It follows from *contraction-extensionality* that $A+\neg\neg\alpha = A+\alpha$, and from *contraction-inclusion* that $A+\alpha \subseteq A$. We therefore have:
$A+\alpha \subseteq A\cap\mathrm{Cn}((A+\alpha)\cup\{\neg\alpha\})$
$= A\cap\mathrm{Cn}((A+\neg\neg\alpha)\cup\{\neg\alpha\})$
$= A+'\alpha$.

c. We only need *inclusion* and *extensionality*. *Closure*, *vacuity*, and *success* are not needed for this result.

d. Suppose to the contrary that $A+''\alpha \not\subseteq A+'\alpha$ for some α. Then there is some ε such that $\varepsilon \in A+''\alpha$ and $\varepsilon \notin A+'\alpha$. Since +'' satisfies *contraction-inclusion*, it follows from $\varepsilon \in A+''\alpha$ that $\varepsilon \in A$. It follows from Observations 3.54 and 3.55 that +' satisfies *recovery*, and thus $\varepsilon \in \mathrm{Cn}((A+'\alpha)\cup\{\alpha\})$. Furthermore, +' satisfies *contraction-closure*, and we can conclude from $\varepsilon \notin A+'\alpha$ that $\varepsilon \notin \mathrm{Cn}(A+'\alpha)$. It follows from $\varepsilon \in \mathrm{Cn}((A+'\alpha)\cup\{\alpha\})$ and $\varepsilon \notin \mathrm{Cn}(A+'\alpha)$ that $\varepsilon \notin \mathrm{Cn}((A+'\alpha)\cup\{\neg\alpha\})$.

We know from Part *a* of the present exercise that + and +' are revision-equivalent. By assumption, so are + and +'', and thus so are +' and +''. Thus, $\mathrm{Cn}((A+'\neg\neg\alpha)\cup\{\neg\alpha\}) = \mathrm{Cn}((A+''\neg\neg\alpha)\cup\{\neg\alpha\})$, i.e. (by *contraction-extensionality*) $\mathrm{Cn}((A+'\alpha)\cup\{\neg\alpha\}) = \mathrm{Cn}((A+''\alpha)\cup\{\neg\alpha\})$. This, however, is impossible. We have just shown that $\varepsilon \notin \mathrm{Cn}((A+'\alpha)\cup\{\neg\alpha\})$, and it follows from $\varepsilon \in A+''\alpha$ that $\varepsilon \in \mathrm{Cn}((A+''\alpha)\cup\{\neg\alpha\})$. We can conclude from this contradiction that $A+''\alpha \subseteq A+'\alpha$ for all α.

176. *(a) to (b)*: Let (a) be satisfied, and let $\beta \in A\ddagger_\gamma\alpha$. We need to show that $A\ddagger_\gamma\alpha \subseteq A\ddagger_\gamma(\alpha\&\beta))$
$\beta \in A\ddagger_\gamma\alpha$
$\beta \in \mathrm{Cn}((A\sim_\gamma\neg\alpha)\cup\{\alpha\})$ (Levi identity)
$\alpha\rightarrow\beta \in \mathrm{Cn}(A\sim_\gamma\neg\alpha)$ (deduction property)
$\alpha\rightarrow\beta \in A\sim_\gamma\neg\alpha$ (*contraction-closure*)
$\alpha\rightarrow\beta \in A\sim_\gamma((\neg\alpha\vee\neg\beta)\&(\alpha\rightarrow\beta))$ (*contraction-extensionality*)
$A\sim_\gamma((\neg\alpha\vee\neg\beta)\&(\alpha\rightarrow\beta)) \subseteq A\sim_\gamma(\neg\alpha\vee\neg\beta)$ (from (a))
$A\sim_\gamma\neg\alpha \subseteq A\sim_\gamma(\neg(\alpha\&\beta))$ (*contraction-extensionality*)
$\mathrm{Cn}((A\sim_\gamma\neg\alpha)\cup\{\alpha\}) \subseteq \mathrm{Cn}((A\sim_\gamma(\neg(\alpha\&\beta)))\cup\{\alpha\&\beta\})$ (property of Cn)
$A\ddagger_\gamma\alpha \subseteq A\ddagger_\gamma(\alpha\&\beta)$ (Levi identity)

(b) to (a): Let (b) be satisfied, and let $\beta \in A\sim_\gamma(\alpha\&\beta)$. We need to show that $A\sim_\gamma(\alpha\&\beta) \subseteq A\sim_\gamma\alpha$.
$\beta \in A\sim_\gamma(\alpha\&\beta)$
$\beta \in A\cap(A\ddagger_\gamma\neg(\alpha\&\beta))$ (Harper identity)
$\beta \in A\ddagger_\gamma\neg(\alpha\&\beta)$
$\alpha\rightarrow\beta \in A\ddagger_\gamma\neg(\alpha\&\beta)$ (*revision-closure*)
$A\ddagger_\gamma\neg(\alpha\&\beta) \subseteq A\ddagger_\gamma(\neg(\alpha\&\beta)\&(\alpha\rightarrow\beta))$ (*cautious monotony*)
$A\ddagger_\gamma\neg(\alpha\&\beta) \subseteq A\ddagger_\gamma\neg\alpha$ (*revision-extensionality*)
$A\cap(A\ddagger_\gamma\neg(\alpha\&\beta)) \subseteq A\cap(A\ddagger_\gamma\neg\alpha)$
$A\sim_\gamma(\alpha\&\beta) \subseteq A\sim_\gamma\alpha$ (Harper identity)

177. *(a) implies (b)*: Suppose that *reciprocity* holds and that $\beta\rightarrow\alpha \in A\sim_\gamma\alpha$ and $\alpha\rightarrow\beta \in A\sim_\gamma\beta$. It follows from *contraction-closure* that $\neg\alpha\rightarrow\neg\beta \in A\sim_\gamma\alpha$, by the deduction property that $\neg\beta \in \mathrm{Cn}((A\sim_\gamma\alpha)\cup\{\neg\alpha\})$, by *contraction-extensionality* that $\neg\beta \in \mathrm{Cn}((A\sim_\gamma\neg\neg\alpha)\cup\{\neg\alpha\})$, and by the Levi identity that $\neg\beta \in A\ddagger_\gamma\neg\alpha$. In the same way it follows that $\neg\alpha \in A\ddagger_\gamma\neg\beta$, and we can conclude from *reciprocity* that $A\ddagger_{\gamma}\neg\alpha = A\ddagger_{\gamma}\neg\beta$. It follows from this that $A\cap(A\ddagger_{\gamma}\neg\alpha) = A\cap(A\ddagger_{\gamma}\neg\beta)$, and thus by the Harper identity that $A\sim_{\gamma}\alpha = A\sim_{\gamma}\beta$.

(b) implies (a): Let (b) hold. For one direction of *reciprocity*, let $A\ddagger_{\gamma}\alpha = A\ddagger_{\gamma}\beta$. It follows from *revision-success* that $\beta \in A\ddagger_{\gamma}\beta$ and hence $\beta \in A\ddagger_{\gamma}\alpha$. In the same way, it follows that $\alpha \in A\ddagger_{\gamma}\beta$. (Note that (2) is not needed for this part of the proof.)

For the other direction of *reciprocity*, let $\beta \in A\ddagger_{\gamma}\alpha$ and $\alpha \in A\ddagger_{\gamma}\beta$. We then have:

$\beta \in A\ddagger_{\gamma}\alpha$ and $\alpha \in A\ddagger_{\gamma}\beta$

$\beta \in \mathrm{Cn}((A\sim_{\gamma}\neg\alpha)\cup\{\alpha\})$ and $\alpha \in \mathrm{Cn}((A\sim_{\gamma}\neg\beta)\cup\{\beta\})$ (Levi identity)

$\alpha\rightarrow\beta \in \mathrm{Cn}(A\sim_{\gamma}\neg\alpha)$ and $\beta\rightarrow\alpha \in \mathrm{Cn}(A\sim_{\gamma}\neg\beta)$

$\neg\beta\rightarrow\neg\alpha \in \mathrm{Cn}(A\sim_{\gamma}\neg\alpha)$ and $\neg\alpha\rightarrow\neg\beta \in \mathrm{Cn}(A\sim_{\gamma}\neg\beta)$

$\neg\beta\rightarrow\neg\alpha \in A\sim_{\gamma}\neg\alpha$ and $\neg\alpha\rightarrow\neg\beta \in A\sim_{\gamma}\neg\beta$ (*contraction-closure*)

$A\sim_{\gamma}\neg\alpha = A\sim_{\gamma}\neg\beta$ (from (b))

From this and $\alpha\rightarrow\beta \in \mathrm{Cn}(A\sim_{\gamma}\neg\alpha)$ and $\beta\rightarrow\alpha \in \mathrm{Cn}(A\sim_{\gamma}\neg\beta)$ (also shown above) it follows that that $\alpha\leftrightarrow\beta \in \mathrm{Cn}(A\sim_{\gamma}\neg\alpha)$. Hence:

$A\ddagger_{\gamma}\alpha = \mathrm{Cn}((A\sim_{\gamma}\neg\alpha)\cup\{\alpha\})$

$= \mathrm{Cn}((A\sim_{\gamma}\neg\alpha)\cup\{\beta\})$

$= \mathrm{Cn}((A\sim_{\gamma}\neg\beta)\cup\{\beta\})$

$= A\ddagger_{\gamma}\beta$

178. Let $\mathbb{R}(+_m) = *_m$ and $\mathbb{R}(\sim) = \ddagger$. It follows from the Levi identity that:

(i) If $\neg\alpha \in A$, then $A*_m\alpha = \mathrm{Cn}(\{\alpha\})$.

(ii) If $\neg\alpha \notin A$, then $A*_m\alpha = \mathrm{Cn}(A\cup\{\alpha\})$

If follows from Observation 3.21 that $*_m$ coincides with $\ddagger$.

179. There are three cases.

Case 1, α is inconsistent. Then $\alpha\vee\beta$ is equivalent with β, and it follows from *extensionality* that $A*(\alpha\vee\beta) = A*\beta$.

Case 2, β is inconsistent. It follows in the same way that $A*(\alpha\vee\beta) = A*\alpha$.

Case 3, both α and β are consistent. Then $\alpha\vee\beta$ is also consistent. It follows from Observation 3.22 that $A*\alpha$, $A*\beta$ and $A*(\alpha\vee\beta)$ are all maximally consistent subsets of $\mathcal{L}$, i.e. they are all elements of $\mathcal{L}\perp\!\!\perp$.

It follows from *success* that $\alpha\vee\beta \in A*(\alpha\vee\beta)$ and from *consistency* that either $\neg\alpha \notin A*(\alpha\vee\beta)$ or $\neg\beta \notin A*(\alpha\vee\beta)$.

If $\neg\alpha \notin A*(\alpha\vee\beta)$, then it follows from *disjunctive inclusion* that $A*(\alpha\vee\beta) \subseteq A*\alpha$. Since both $A*(\alpha\vee\beta)$ and $A*\alpha$ are elements of $\mathcal{L}\perp\!\!\perp$, $A*(\alpha\vee\beta) \not\subset A*\alpha$ and thus $A*(\alpha\vee\beta) = A*\alpha$.

If $\neg\beta \notin A*(\alpha\vee\beta)$, then it follows in the same way that $A*(\alpha\vee\beta) = A*\beta$.

180. a. Let $W \in \mathcal{L}\perp\perp$. Then it holds for all sentences α that either $\alpha \in W$ or $\neg\alpha \in W$, but not both. (Cf. Observation 1.57). Thus, $W \in [\alpha]$ if and only if $W \notin [\neg\alpha]$.
b. For one direction, let $A \subseteq B$ and $W \in [B]$. Then $B \subseteq W$, and consequently $A \subseteq W$ so that $W \in [A]$.
For the other direction, suppose that $[B] \subseteq [A]$. Then $\cap[A] \subseteq \cap[B]$, i.e., $A \subseteq B$.
c. $X \in [\text{Cn}(A \cup B)]$
iff $\text{Cn}(A \cup B) \subseteq X \in \mathcal{L}\perp\perp$.
iff $\text{Cn}(A) \subseteq X \in \mathcal{L}\perp\perp$ and $\text{Cn}(B) \subseteq X \in \mathcal{L}\perp\perp$
iff $X \in [A]$ and $X \in [B]$
iff $X \in [A] \cap [B]$
d. It follows from Part *b* that $[A] \subseteq [A \cap B]$ and $[B] \subseteq [A \cap B]$.
e. $[\alpha] \subseteq [\beta]$
iff $[\text{Cn}(\{\alpha\})] \subseteq [\text{Cn}(\{\beta\})]$
iff $\text{Cn}(\{\beta\}) \subseteq \text{Cn}(\{\alpha\})$ (Part *b* of this exercise)
iff $\vdash \alpha \rightarrow \beta$
f. $[\alpha \& \beta] = [\text{Cn}(\{\alpha \& \beta\})]$
$= [\text{Cn}(\text{Cn}(\{\alpha\}) \cup \text{Cn}(\{\beta\}))]$
$= [\text{Cn}(\{\alpha\})] \cap [\text{Cn}(\{\beta\})]$ (Part *c* of this exercise)
$= [\alpha] \cap [\beta]$
g. For one direction, let $W \in [\alpha \vee \beta]$. Then $\alpha \vee \beta \in W \in \mathcal{L}\perp\perp$, and we can conclude from Observation 1.57 that either $\alpha \in W$ or $\beta \in W$. In the first case, $W \in [\alpha]$, and in the second case $W \in [\beta]$. Thus, in both cases $W \in [\alpha] \cup [\beta]$.
For the other direction, let $W \in [\alpha] \cup [\beta]$. Then either $W \in [\alpha]$ or $W \in [\beta]$, so that either $\alpha \in W$ or $\beta \in W$, and thus in both cases $\alpha \vee \beta \in W$, so that $W \in [\alpha \vee \beta]$.
h. $[\alpha \rightarrow \beta] = [\neg\alpha \vee \beta]$ (sentential logic)
$= [\neg\alpha] \cup [\beta]$ (Part *g* of this exercise)
i. $[\alpha \rightarrow \beta] \cap [\beta \rightarrow \alpha]$
$= [(\alpha \rightarrow \beta) \& (\beta \rightarrow \alpha)]$ (Part *f* of this exercise)
$= [(\alpha \& \beta) \vee (\neg\alpha \& \neg\beta)]$ (sentential logic)
$= [\alpha \& \beta] \cup [\neg\alpha \& \neg\beta]$ (Part *g* of this exercise)

181. We have $[\text{Cn}(A)] = [\&A]$, and since $\&A$ is logically equivalent to $\neg n(A)$ the rest follows from Part *a* of Exercise 180.

182. a. $\mathcal{W} \circledast [\alpha] = \mathcal{W} \oplus [\neg\alpha] \oplus [\alpha]$.
b. $\mathcal{W} \oplus [\alpha] = \mathcal{W} \cup (\mathcal{W} \circledast [\neg\alpha])$.

183. a. An operator $\circledast$ of propositional revision such that $\mathcal{W} \circledast [\alpha]$ is a singleton (consists of a single possible world) if $\mathcal{W} \subseteq [\neg\alpha]$.

b. The operator $\circledast$ of propositional revision such that $\mathcal{W}\circledast[\alpha] = [\alpha]$ if $\mathcal{W} \subseteq [\neg\alpha]$.

184. a. $[\beta]\cap S_\alpha \neq \varnothing$ means that S_α intersects with $[\beta]$. Since S_β is a subset of all spheres that intersect with $[\beta]$, it follows directly that $S_\beta \subseteq S_\alpha$.
b. It follows from $\vdash\alpha\rightarrow\beta$ that $[\alpha] \subseteq [\beta]$ (Exercise 52), and thus from $[\alpha]\cap S_\alpha \neq \varnothing$ that $[\beta]\cap S_\alpha \neq \varnothing$. We can conclude as in Part *a* that $S_\beta \subseteq S_\alpha$.
c. Directly from Part *a*.

185. We have for all α: $\mathrm{Cn}((A+_R\neg\alpha)\cup\{\alpha\}) \subseteq \mathrm{Cn}((A+\neg\alpha)\cup\{\alpha\}) \subseteq \mathrm{Cn}((A+_G\neg\alpha)\cup\{\alpha\})$. Since $+_R$ and $+_G$ are revision-equivalent (Part 1 of Observation 3.28), it follows that $\mathbb{R}(+) = \mathbb{R}(+_G) = \mathbb{R}(+_R)$, and the desired result therefore follows from Part 2 of Observation 3.28.

SOLUTIONS FOR CHAPTER 4$^+$

186. *Inclusion* ($A+\alpha \subseteq A$): Suppose that *inclusion* holds for the operator $-$ on B. Let $\mathbf{K} = \mathrm{Cn}(B)$ and let $+$ be the closure of $-$. In order to show that *inclusion* holds for $\mathbf{K}$, we must show that $\mathbf{K}+\alpha \subseteq \mathbf{K}$ holds for all α.

Since *inclusion* holds for B, we have $B-\alpha \subseteq B$, and consequently $\mathrm{Cn}(B-\alpha) \subseteq \mathrm{Cn}(B)$. Since $\mathbf{K}+\alpha = \mathrm{Cn}(B-\alpha)$ and $\mathbf{K} = \mathrm{Cn}(B)$, it follows directly that $\mathbf{K}+\alpha \subseteq \mathbf{K}$.

Success (If $\alpha \notin \mathrm{Cn}(\varnothing)$, then $\alpha \notin \mathrm{Cn}(A+\alpha)$): Suppose that *success* holds for the operator $-$ on B. Let $\mathbf{K} = \mathrm{Cn}(B)$ and let $+$ be the closure of $-$. In order to show that *success* holds for $\mathbf{K}$, we must show that if $\alpha \notin \mathrm{Cn}(\varnothing)$, then $\alpha \notin \mathrm{Cn}(\mathbf{K}+\alpha)$.

Let $\alpha \notin \mathrm{Cn}(\varnothing)$. Since *success* holds for B, we then have $\alpha \notin \mathrm{Cn}(B-\alpha)$, and since $\mathrm{Cn}(B-\alpha) = \mathrm{Cn}(\mathbf{K}+\alpha)$ it follows that $\alpha \notin \mathrm{Cn}(\mathbf{K}+\alpha)$.

Extensionality (If $\alpha\leftrightarrow\beta \in \mathrm{Cn}(\varnothing)$, then $A+\alpha = A+\beta$.): Suppose that *extensionality* holds for the operator $-$ on B. Let $\mathbf{K} = \mathrm{Cn}(B)$ and let $+$ be the closure of $-$. In order to show that *extensionality* holds for $\mathbf{K}$, we must show that if $\alpha\leftrightarrow\beta \in \mathrm{Cn}(\varnothing)$, then $\mathbf{K}+\alpha = \mathbf{K}+\beta$.

Let $\alpha\leftrightarrow\beta \in \mathrm{Cn}(\varnothing)$. Since $-$ satisfies *extensionality*, we then have $B-\alpha = B-\beta$, and consequently $\mathrm{Cn}(B-\alpha) = \mathrm{Cn}(B-\beta)$, i.e., $\mathbf{K}+\alpha = \mathbf{K}+\beta$.

Failure (If $\alpha \in \mathrm{Cn}(\varnothing)$, then $A+\alpha = A$.): Suppose that *failure* holds for the operator $-$ on B. Let $\mathbf{K} = \mathrm{Cn}(B)$ and let $+$ be the closure of $-$. In order to show that *failure* holds for $\mathbf{K}$, we must show that if $\alpha \in \mathrm{Cn}(\varnothing)$, then $\mathbf{K}+\alpha = \mathbf{K}$.

It follows from $\alpha \in \mathrm{Cn}(\varnothing)$, since $-$ satisfies *failure*, that $B-\alpha = B$, and consequently $\mathrm{Cn}(B-\alpha) = \mathrm{Cn}(B)$, i.e., $\mathbf{K}+\alpha = \mathbf{K}$.

187. *Conservativity*: Let $\mathbf{K} = \mathrm{Cn}(B)$ and let $+$ be the closure of the operator $-$ on B. Suppose that $-$ satisfies *conservativity*. In order to show that $+$ satisfies *conservativity*, suppose that $\mathbf{K}+\beta \not\subseteq \mathbf{K}+\alpha$. We need to show that there is some δ such that $\mathbf{K}+\alpha \subseteq \mathbf{K}+\delta \nvdash \alpha$ and $\mathbf{K}+\delta \cup \mathbf{K}+\beta \vdash \alpha$.

It follows from $\mathbf{K}+\beta \not\subseteq \mathbf{K}+\alpha$ that $B-\beta \not\subseteq B-\alpha$. Since $-$ satisfies *conservativity*, there is some δ such that $B-\alpha \subseteq B-\delta \nvdash \alpha$ and $B-\delta \cup B-\beta \vdash \alpha$. It follows that $\mathbf{K}+\alpha \subseteq \mathbf{K}+\delta \nvdash \alpha$ and $\mathbf{K}+\delta \cup \mathbf{K}+\beta \vdash \alpha$.

Strong conservativity: Let $\mathbf{K} = \mathrm{Cn}(B)$ and let $+$ be the closure of the operator $-$ on B. Suppose that $-$ satisfies *strong conservativity*. In order to show that $+$ satisfies *strong conservativity*, suppose that $\mathbf{K}+\beta \not\subseteq \mathbf{K}+\alpha$. We need to show that $\mathbf{K}+\alpha \nvdash \alpha$ and $\mathbf{K}+\beta \cup \mathbf{K}+\alpha \vdash \alpha$.

It follows from $\mathbf{K}+\beta \not\subseteq \mathbf{K}+\alpha$ that $B-\beta \not\subseteq B-\alpha$. Since $-$ satisfies *strong conservativity*, $B-\alpha \nvdash \alpha$ and $B-\beta \cup B-\alpha \vdash \alpha$. It follows that $\mathbf{K}+\alpha \subseteq \nvdash \alpha$ and $\mathbf{K}+\beta \cup \mathbf{K}+\alpha \vdash \alpha$.

188. Let $\mathbf{K} = \mathrm{Cn}(B)$, and let $+$ be the closure of the operator $-$ for B.
a. Since $-$ satisfies *conjunctive covering*, it holds for all sentences α and β that either $B-(\alpha\&\beta) \subseteq B-\alpha$ or $B-(\alpha\&\beta) \subseteq B-\beta$. In the first case it follows that $\mathbf{K}+(\alpha\&\beta) = \mathbf{K}+\alpha$ and in the second case that $\mathbf{K}+(\alpha\&\beta) = \mathbf{K}+\alpha$.
b. Let $-$ satisfy the postulate, and let $\beta \in \mathrm{Cn}(\mathbf{K}+(\alpha\&\beta))$. We then have $\beta \in \mathrm{Cn}(B-(\alpha\&\beta))$. Since $-$ satisfies the postulate it follows that $B-(\alpha\&\beta) \subseteq B-\alpha$, and consequently $\mathrm{Cn}(B-(\alpha\&\beta)) \subseteq \mathrm{Cn}(B-\alpha)$, i.e., $\mathbf{K}+(\alpha\&\beta) \subseteq \mathbf{K}+\alpha$.
c. Since $-$ satisfies *weak conjunctive inclusion*, we have for all sentences α and β:
$B-(\alpha\&\beta) \subseteq \mathrm{Cn}((B-\alpha)\cup(B-\beta))$
$\mathrm{Cn}(B-(\alpha\&\beta)) \subseteq \mathrm{Cn}((B-\alpha)\cup(B-\beta))$
$\mathrm{Cn}(B-(\alpha\&\beta)) \subseteq \mathrm{Cn}(\mathrm{Cn}(B-\alpha)\cup\mathrm{Cn}(B-\beta))$
$\mathbf{K}+(\alpha\&\beta) \subseteq \mathrm{Cn}((\mathbf{K}+\alpha)\cup(\mathbf{K}+\beta))$

189. For one direction, suppose that *finitude* is satisfied. Then there is a finite set A such that for every α, $\mathbf{K}+\alpha = \mathrm{Cn}(A')$ for some $A' \subseteq A$. Since every subset of A is finite, *finite representability* holds. Since A only has a finite number of subsets, *finite number of contractions* holds as well.

For the other direction, suppose that *finite representability* and *finite number of contractions* hold. Let $\mathbf{K}_1 ... \mathbf{K}_n$ be all the possible outcomes of contractions. For each $\mathbf{K}_k$, with $1 \leq k \leq n$, there is a finite set A_k such that $\mathbf{K}_k = \mathrm{Cn}(A_k)$. Let $A = A_1 \cup ... \cup A_n$. Then A is the finite set that is needed for *finitude* to hold.

190. a. Let $\mathbf{K} = \mathrm{Cn}(B)$ and let $+$ be the closure of the operator $-$ on B. Let $-$ satisfy *hyperregularity*. In order to show that $+$ satisfies the same postulate, suppose that $\vdash \alpha\rightarrow\beta$ and $\mathbf{K}+\alpha \nvdash \beta$. We then have $B-\alpha \nvdash \beta$, and since $-$ satisfies *hyperregularity* it follows that $B-\alpha = B-\beta$, from which $\mathbf{K}+\alpha = \mathbf{K}+\beta$ follows directly.
b. Let A be a set and $\sim_\gamma$ a TMR maxichoice contraction on A. Let $\sqsubseteq$ be the marking-off relation by which γ is TMR. Furthermore, suppose that $\vdash \alpha\rightarrow\beta$ and $A\sim_\gamma\alpha \nvdash \beta$. We have to show that $A\sim_\gamma\beta = A\sim_\gamma\alpha$.

Since $\sim_\gamma$ is maxichoice, $A\sim_\gamma\alpha \in A\perp\alpha$. It therefore follows from $\vdash \alpha\rightarrow\beta$ and $A\sim_\gamma\alpha \nvdash \beta$ that $A\sim_\gamma\alpha \in A\perp\beta$.

Let $X \in A\perp\beta$. It follows from $\vdash \alpha\rightarrow\beta$ that $X \nvdash \alpha$. Therefore, there is some X' such that $X \subseteq X' \in A\perp\alpha$.

It follows from $X' \in A\perp\alpha$ and $A\sim_\gamma\alpha \in \gamma(A\perp\alpha)$ that $X' \sqsubseteq A\sim_\gamma\alpha$. If $X = X'$, then $X \sqsubseteq A\sim_\gamma\alpha$ follows directly. If $X \subset X'$, then it follows by the maximizing property that $X \sqsubseteq X'$, and thus from the transitivity of $\sqsubseteq$ that $X \sqsubseteq A\sim_\gamma\alpha$.

Thus, $X \subseteq A\sim_\gamma\alpha$ for all $X \in A\perp\beta$. Since $A\sim_\gamma\alpha \in A\perp\beta$, we can conclude $A\sim_\gamma\alpha \in \gamma(A\perp\beta)$, and, since $\sim_\gamma$ is maxichoice, that $A\sim_\gamma\alpha = A\sim_\gamma\beta$.

191. Suppose to the contrary that the three conditions are satisfied for α and β with respect to an operator +. Since α and β are elements of the logically closed set **K**, so is $\alpha\rightarrow\beta$. It follows from *recovery* that $\mathbf{K}+(\alpha\rightarrow\beta) \vdash (\alpha\rightarrow\beta)\rightarrow\alpha$, or equivalently $\mathbf{K}+(\alpha\rightarrow\beta) \vdash \alpha$. It follows from $\mathbf{K}+(\alpha\rightarrow\beta) \vdash \alpha$, using the third condition (antecedent of symmetry) that $\mathbf{K}+(\alpha\rightarrow\beta) \vdash \beta$. Since $\alpha\rightarrow\beta$ follows logically from α and β, we now have $\mathbf{K}+(\alpha\rightarrow\beta) \vdash (\alpha\rightarrow\beta)$, and *success* yields $\alpha\rightarrow\beta \in \mathrm{Cn}(\varnothing)$.

In the same way it follows that $\beta\rightarrow\alpha \in \mathrm{Cn}(\varnothing)$. Hence, $\alpha\leftrightarrow\beta \in \mathrm{Cn}(\varnothing)$, contrary to the conditions. This contradiction concludes the proof.

192. Since – satisfies *meet identity*, it holds for all sentences α and β that:
$B-(\alpha\&\beta) = (B-\alpha)\cap(B-\beta)$
$\mathrm{Cn}(B-(\alpha\&\beta)) = \mathrm{Cn}((B-\alpha)\cap(B-\beta))$
$\mathrm{Cn}(B-(\alpha\&\beta)) = \mathrm{Cn}(B-\alpha)\cap\mathrm{Cn}(B-\beta))$ (Observation 1.34)
$\mathbf{K}+(\alpha\&\beta) = (\mathbf{K}+\alpha)\cap(\mathbf{K}+\beta)$
(*Inclusion* and *relative closure* are needed for the application of Observation 1.34.)

193. Let $\mathbf{K} = \mathrm{Cn}(B)$, and let + be the closure of the operator – for B.

Since – satisfies *conjunctive factoring*, it holds for all sentences α and β that either (1) $B-(\alpha\&\beta) = B-\alpha$, (2) $B-(\alpha\&\beta) = B-\beta$, or (3) $B-(\alpha\&\beta) = (B-\alpha) \cap (B-\beta)$.

In case (1) it follows directly that $\mathbf{K}+(\alpha\&\beta) = \mathbf{K}+\alpha$, and similarly in case (2) that $\mathbf{K}+(\alpha\&\beta) = \mathbf{K}+\alpha$. In case (3):
$\mathbf{K}+(\alpha\&\beta)$
$= \mathrm{Cn}(B-(\alpha\&\beta))$
$= \mathrm{Cn}((B-\alpha)\cap(B-\beta))$ (by assumption, see above)
$= \mathrm{Cn}(B-\alpha)\cap\mathrm{Cn}(B-\beta)$ (Observation 1.34)
$= (\mathbf{K}+\alpha) \cap (\mathbf{K}+\beta)$

194. a. It follows directly from the definition of closure of operators (Definition 4.1) that if $B-\alpha \subseteq B-\beta$, then $\mathbf{K}+\alpha \subseteq \mathbf{K}+\beta$.

For the other direction, suppose to the contrary that there are α and β such that $\mathbf{K}+\alpha \subseteq \mathbf{K}+\beta$ and $B-\alpha \not\subseteq B-\beta$. It follows from *inclusion* that $B-\alpha \subseteq B$, and thus $B-\alpha \subseteq B\cap(\mathbf{K}+\alpha)$. It follows from *relative closure* that $B\cap(\mathbf{K}+\alpha) \subseteq B-\alpha$. We can conclude that $B-\alpha = B\cap(\mathbf{K}+\alpha)$. In the same way it follows that $B-\beta = B\cap(\mathbf{K}+\beta)$.

We thus have $B\cap(\mathbf{K}+\alpha) \not\subseteq B\cap(\mathbf{K}+\beta)$. However, it follows from $\mathbf{K}+\alpha \subseteq \mathbf{K}+\beta$ that $B\cap(\mathbf{K}+\alpha) \subseteq B\cap(\mathbf{K}+\beta)$. This contradiction concludes the proof.

b. $\mathbf{K}+\alpha = \mathbf{K}+\beta$
iff $\mathbf{K}+\alpha \subseteq \mathbf{K}+\beta$ and $\mathbf{K}+\beta \subseteq \mathbf{K}+\alpha$
iff $B-\alpha \subseteq B-\beta$ and $B-\beta \subseteq B-\alpha$ (Part *a* of this exercise)
iff $B-\alpha = B-\beta$
c. $\mathbf{K}+\alpha \subset \mathbf{K}+\beta$
iff $\mathbf{K}+\alpha \subseteq \mathbf{K}+\beta$ and $\mathbf{K}+\beta \not\subseteq \mathbf{K}+\alpha$
iff $B-\alpha \subseteq B-\beta$ and $B-\beta \not\subseteq B-\alpha$ (Part *a* of this exercise)
iff $B-\alpha \subset B-\beta$

195. Let $(B-\alpha_1)\cap\ldots\cap(B-\alpha_n) \subseteq (B-\beta)$, and $\delta \in (\mathbf{K}+\alpha_1)\cap\ldots\cap(\mathbf{K}+\alpha_n)$ Then:
$\delta \in \mathrm{Cn}(B-\alpha_1)\cap\ldots\cap\mathrm{Cn}(B-\alpha_n)$
$\delta \in \mathrm{Cn}((B-\alpha_1)\cap\ldots\cap(B-\alpha_n))$ (Observation 1.34)
$\delta \in \mathrm{Cn}(B-\beta)$
$\delta \in \mathbf{K}+\beta$

196. If $\vdash \neg\alpha$, then $B\sim_\gamma\neg\alpha = B\vec{\sim}_\gamma\neg\alpha$, from which the desired conclusion follows directly.

If $\nvdash \neg\alpha$, then:
$\mathrm{Cn}((B\vec{\sim}_\gamma\neg\alpha)\cup\{\alpha\})$
$= \mathrm{Cn}(\cap\gamma(B\perp\neg\alpha) \cup \{\neg\alpha\rightarrow\&B\} \cup \{\alpha\})$
$= \mathrm{Cn}(\cap\gamma(B\perp\neg\alpha) \cup \{\alpha\})$ (since α implies $\neg\alpha\rightarrow\&B$)
$= \mathrm{Cn}((B\sim_\gamma\neg\alpha) \cup \{\alpha\})$

197. We know from Observation 2.12 that $\mathbf{K}\sim\alpha = \mathbf{K}\cap\mathrm{Cn}(\{\neg\alpha\})$.

First step: We are going to show that $\varepsilon \in \mathbf{K}\cap\mathrm{Cn}(\{\neg\alpha\})$ if and only if ε is equivalent with $\alpha\rightarrow\beta$ for some $\beta \in \mathbf{K}$.

One direction: If $\beta \in \mathbf{K}$ then, since $\mathbf{K}$ is logically closed, $\alpha\rightarrow\beta \in \mathbf{K}$. Since $\alpha\rightarrow\beta \in \mathrm{Cn}(\{\neg\alpha\})$, we also have $\alpha\rightarrow\beta \in \mathbf{K}\cap\mathrm{Cn}(\{\neg\alpha\})$, and since $\mathbf{K}\cap\mathrm{Cn}(\{\neg\alpha\})$ is logically closed, it holds for every sentence ε that if ε is equivalent with $\alpha\rightarrow\beta$, then $\varepsilon \in \mathbf{K}\cap\mathrm{Cn}(\{\neg\alpha\})$.

The other direction: Let $\varepsilon \in \mathbf{K}\cap\mathrm{Cn}(\{\neg\alpha\})$. It follows from $\vdash \neg\alpha\rightarrow\varepsilon$ that $\vdash \varepsilon\leftrightarrow(\alpha\rightarrow\varepsilon)$. Let $\beta = \varepsilon$, and we are done.

Second step:
+ satisfies *recovery*
iff $\mathbf{K} \subseteq \mathrm{Cn}((\mathbf{K}+\alpha)\cup\{\alpha\})$
iff for all β: if $\beta \in \mathbf{K}$ then $\beta \in \mathrm{Cn}((\mathbf{K}+\alpha)\cup\{\alpha\})$
iff for all β: if $\beta \in \mathbf{K}$ then $\alpha\rightarrow\beta \in \mathrm{Cn}(\mathbf{K}\div\alpha)$
iff for all β: if $\beta \in \mathbf{K}$ then $\alpha\rightarrow\beta \in \mathrm{Cn}(B-\alpha)$
iff $\{\alpha\rightarrow\beta \mid \beta \in \mathbf{K}\} \subseteq \mathrm{Cn}(B-\alpha)$
iff $\mathbf{K}\sim\alpha \subseteq \mathrm{Cn}(B-\alpha)$ (here step 1 of the proof is used)

198. a. If $\mathbf{K}$ is inconsistent, then there is no ξ such that $\xi \notin \mathbf{K}$.

b. Let $\xi \in \text{Cn}(\varnothing)$. It follows from *failure* that $\mathbf{K}+\xi = \mathbf{K}$ and from *finitude* that $\&(\mathbf{K}+\xi) = \&\mathbf{K}$ is well-defined. We therefore have that $\&\mathbf{K} \in B$, and consequently $\text{Cn}(\{\&\mathbf{K}\}) \subseteq \text{Cn}(B)$, i.e., Thus, $\mathbf{K} \subseteq \text{Cn}(B)$.

It follows from *inclusion* that $B \subseteq \mathbf{K}$, and thus $\text{Cn}(B) \subseteq \mathbf{K}$. We can conclude that $\text{Cn}(B) = \mathbf{K}$.

199. The adjusted list is still an axiomatic characterization of base-generated full meet contraction. Where *conservativity* is used in the proof, *weak conservativity* is sufficient.

200. *(1) to (2)*: Suppose that $\div$ is generated by the kernel contraction $\approx_\sigma$ on a base B for $\mathbf{K}$. According to Definition 2.35, it holds for all α that $B \hat{\approx}_\sigma \alpha = B \cap \text{Cn}(B \approx_\sigma \alpha) = B \cap \text{Cn}(B \setminus \sigma(A \perp\!\!\!\perp \alpha))$. We are going to show that $\text{Cn}(B \hat{\approx}_\sigma \alpha) = \text{Cn}(B \approx_\sigma \alpha)$.

It follows from $B \setminus \sigma(A \perp\!\!\!\perp \alpha) \subseteq B \cap \text{Cn}(B \setminus \sigma(A \perp\!\!\!\perp \alpha))$ that $\text{Cn}(B \setminus \sigma(A \perp\!\!\!\perp \alpha)) \subseteq \text{Cn}(B \cap \text{Cn}(B \setminus \sigma(A \perp\!\!\!\perp \alpha)))$, i.e. $\text{Cn}(B \approx_\sigma \alpha) \subseteq \text{Cn}(B \hat{\approx}_\sigma \alpha)$.

It follows from $B \cap \text{Cn}(B \setminus \sigma(A \perp\!\!\!\perp \alpha)) \subseteq \text{Cn}(B \setminus \sigma(A \perp\!\!\!\perp \alpha))$ that $\text{Cn}(B \cap \text{Cn}(B \setminus \sigma(A \perp\!\!\!\perp \alpha))) \subseteq \text{Cn}(B \setminus \sigma(A \perp\!\!\!\perp \alpha))$, i.e., $\text{Cn}(B \hat{\approx}_\sigma \alpha) \subseteq \text{Cn}(B \approx_\sigma \alpha)$.

Thus, $\text{Cn}(B \hat{\approx}_\sigma \alpha) = \text{Cn}(B \approx_\sigma \alpha)$. According to Theorem 2.36, there is some smooth incision function σ' such that for all α, $B \hat{\approx}_\sigma \alpha = B \approx_{\sigma'} \alpha$.

According to our assumption, it holds for all α that $\mathbf{K}+\alpha = \text{Cn}(B \approx_\sigma \alpha)$. We now have $\mathbf{K}+\alpha = \text{Cn}(B \hat{\approx}_\sigma \alpha) = \text{Cn}(B \approx_{\sigma'} \alpha)$.

(2) implies (1): Every smooth kernel contraction is a kernel contraction.

201. *Part 1*: $\mathcal{V}(A \cap B) \subseteq \mathcal{V}_A(B)$ followd directly from the definition.

By the definition, every element of $\mathcal{V}_A(B)$ is either (1) an element of $\mathcal{V}(A \cap B)$ and thus of $\mathcal{V}(B)$ or (2) a disjunction of a sentence $\alpha \in \mathcal{V}(A \cap B)$ and a sentence $\beta \in \mathcal{V}(B)$. Since both α and β are elements of $\mathcal{V}(B)$, so is $\alpha \vee \beta$.

Part 2: Let $\alpha \in \mathcal{V}(A)$ and $A \subseteq B$. Since $A \subseteq B$, we have $A \cap B = A$ and thus $\alpha \in \mathcal{V}(A \cap B)$, that is, according to the definition, a subset of $\mathcal{V}_A(B)$

Part 3: Let $A \subseteq B$. It follows from Part 2 that $\mathcal{V}(A) \subseteq \mathcal{V}_A(B)$. Thus $\text{Cn}(\mathcal{V}(A)) \subseteq \text{Cn}(\mathcal{V}_A(B))$. Furthermore, it follows from the construction that every element of $\mathcal{V}_A(B)$ is either an element of $\mathcal{V}(A)$ or a disjunction with at least one element of $\mathcal{V}(A)$ as a disjunct, so that $\text{Cn}(\mathcal{V}_A(B)) \subseteq \text{Cn}(\mathcal{V}(A))$.

Thus $\text{Cn}(\mathcal{V}(A)) = \text{Cn}(\mathcal{V}_A(B))$, and since $\text{Cn}(A) = \text{Cn}(\mathcal{V}(A))$ it follows that $\text{Cn}(\mathcal{V}_A(B)) = \text{Cn}(A)$.

Part 4: If $A \cap B = \varnothing$, then $\mathcal{V}(A \cap B) = \varnothing$, from which it follows that $\mathcal{V}_A(B) = \varnothing$.

202. Let $\beta \in \mathcal{V}(B) \setminus \mathcal{V}_A(B)$. It follows from $\beta \in \mathcal{V}(B)$ that $\beta = \beta_1 \vee \ldots \vee \beta_n$ for some $\beta_1, \ldots \beta_n \in B$. Since $\beta \notin \mathcal{V}_A(B)$, none of $\beta_1, \ldots \beta_n$ is an element of $A \cap B$.

It follows that $\{\beta_1,\ldots\beta_n\} \subseteq B\backslash(A\cap B) = B\backslash A$, and consequently that β, the disjunction of $\beta_1,\ldots\beta_n$, is an element of $\mathcal{V}(B\backslash A)$.

203. *PROOF THAT (1) IMPLIES (2)*: Let γ be a selection function such that for all α, $\mathbf{K}{+}\alpha = \text{Cn}(B{\simeq_\gamma}\alpha)$. Since $B{\simeq_\gamma}\alpha$ is logically closed, it follows that for all α, $\mathbf{K}{+}\alpha = B{\simeq_\gamma}\alpha$. Let γ'' be such that

(1) If $\mathcal{V}(B)\perp\alpha \neq \varnothing$, then

$\gamma''(\mathcal{V}(B)\perp\alpha) = \{Y \in \mathcal{V}(B)\perp\alpha \mid \text{Cn}(X) = \text{Cn}(Y) \text{ for some } X \in \gamma(B\perp\alpha)\}$

(2) If $\mathcal{V}(B)\perp\alpha = \varnothing$, then $\gamma''(\mathcal{V}(B)\perp\alpha) = \{\mathcal{V}(B)\}$

Clearly, $\mathcal{V}(B)$ is a finite base for $\mathbf{K}$. We need to show that (I) γ'' is a selection function for $\mathcal{V}(B)$, (II) $\mathbf{K}{+}\alpha \subseteq \text{Cn}(\mathcal{V}(B){\sim_{\gamma''}}\alpha)$, and (III) $\text{Cn}(\mathcal{V}(B){\sim_{\gamma''}}\alpha) \subseteq \mathbf{K}{+}\alpha$.

Part I: In order to show that γ'' is a selection function for $\mathcal{V}(B)$, we need to show that if $\mathcal{V}(B)\perp\alpha \neq \varnothing$, then $\gamma''(\mathcal{V}(B)\perp\alpha) \neq \varnothing$. It follows from $\mathcal{V}(B)\perp\alpha \neq \varnothing$ that α is not a tautology, and thus $B\perp\alpha \neq \varnothing$. Since γ is a selection function, $\gamma(B\perp\alpha)$ is non-empty. Let $X \in \gamma(B\perp\alpha)$. It follows from Observation 4.38 that there is some $Y \in \mathcal{V}(B)\perp\alpha$ such that $\text{Cn}(X) = \text{Cn}(Y)$. It follows from the definition of γ'' that $Y \in \gamma''(\mathcal{V}(B)\perp\alpha)$.

Part II: Let $\beta \in \mathbf{K}{+}\alpha$, i.e., $\beta \in B{\simeq_\gamma}\alpha$. Then for each $X \in \gamma(B\perp\alpha)$, $X \vdash \beta$. By the definition of γ'', for each $Y \in \gamma''(\mathcal{V}(B)\perp\alpha)$, $Y \vdash \beta$. Since the elements of $\mathcal{V}(B)\perp\alpha$ are closed under disjunction, it follows from Observation 1.34 that $\beta \in \text{Cn}(\cap\gamma''(\mathcal{V}(B)\perp\alpha))$, i.e. $\beta \in \text{Cn}(\mathcal{V}(B){\sim_{\gamma''}}\alpha)$.

Part III: Let $\beta \in \text{Cn}(\mathcal{V}(B){\sim_{\gamma''}}\alpha)$, i.e., $\beta \in \text{Cn}(\cap\gamma''(\mathcal{V}(B)\perp\alpha))$. Then for each $Y \in \gamma''(\mathcal{V}(B)\perp\alpha)$ we have $Y \vdash \beta$. By Observation 4.38 and the definition of γ'', for each $X \in \gamma(B\perp\alpha)$ there is some $Y \in \gamma''(\mathcal{V}(B)\perp\alpha)$ such that $\text{Cn}(X) = \text{Cn}(Y)$, and thus $X \vdash \beta$. We may conclude that $\beta \in B{\simeq_\gamma}\alpha$. Thus, $\text{Cn}(\mathcal{V}(B){\sim_{\gamma''}}\alpha) \subseteq B{\simeq_\gamma}\alpha = \mathbf{K}{+}\alpha$.

PROOF THAT (2) IMPLIES (1): Let B be a disjunctively closed base for $\mathbf{K}$ and let γ be a selection function for B that gives rise to the operation $+$ on $\mathbf{K}$, i.e.:

$\mathbf{K}{+}\alpha = \text{Cn}(B{\sim_\gamma}\alpha)$

We are going to use the same base B and the same selection function γ. It is clearly sufficient for the proof to show that $\text{Cn}(B{\sim_\gamma}\alpha) = \text{Cn}(B{\simeq_\gamma}\alpha)$ holds for all α.

In order to show that $\text{Cn}(B{\sim_\gamma}\alpha) \subseteq \text{Cn}(B{\simeq_\gamma}\alpha)$, let $\beta \in \text{Cn}(B{\sim_\gamma}\alpha) = \text{Cn}(\cap\gamma(B\perp\alpha))$. For every $X \in \gamma(B\perp\alpha)$, $\cap\gamma(B\perp\alpha) \subseteq X$, so that $\beta \in \text{Cn}(X)$. It follows that $\beta \in B{\simeq_\gamma}\alpha$, thus $\beta \in \text{Cn}(B{\simeq_\gamma}\alpha)$.

In order to show that $\text{Cn}(B{\simeq_\gamma}\alpha) \subseteq \text{Cn}(B{\sim_\gamma}\alpha)$, let $\beta \in \text{Cn}(B{\simeq_\gamma}\alpha)$. Then for each $X \in \gamma(B\perp\alpha)$, we have $\beta \in \text{Cn}(X)$. It follows from Observation 1.34 that $\beta \in \text{Cn}(\cap\gamma(B\perp\alpha))$, i.e., $\beta \in \text{Cn}(B{\sim_\gamma}\alpha)$.

204. Let B be a base for $\mathbf{K}$ and γ a selection function for B that is transitively maximizingly relational. We know from Observation 2.19 that $\sim_\gamma$ satisfies *conjunctive overlap*, i.e., that $(B\sim_\gamma\alpha)\cap(B\sim_\gamma\beta) \subseteq B\sim_\gamma(\alpha\&\beta)$ for all α and β.

Now let $\mathbf{K}+\delta \subseteq (\mathbf{K}+\alpha)\cap(\mathbf{K}+\beta)$. It follows from $\mathbf{K}+\delta \subseteq \mathbf{K}+\alpha$ that $B\cap(\mathbf{K}+\delta) \subseteq B\cap(\mathbf{K}+\alpha)$, i.e., $B\sim_\gamma\delta \subseteq B\sim_\gamma\alpha$. Similarly, $B\sim_\gamma\delta \subseteq B\sim_\gamma\beta$. Since $(B\sim_\gamma\alpha)\cap(B\sim_\gamma\beta) \subseteq B\sim_\gamma(\alpha\&\beta)$, we have $B\sim_\gamma\delta \subseteq B\sim_\gamma(\alpha\&\beta)$, thus $\mathrm{Cn}(B\sim_\gamma\delta) \subseteq \mathrm{Cn}(B\sim_\gamma(\alpha\&\beta))$, i.e. $\mathbf{K}+\delta \subseteq \mathbf{K}+(\alpha\&\beta)$.

205. Let B be a belief base and $\mathbf{K} = \mathrm{Cn}(B)$. Furthermore, let $\circ$ be an operator on B and $*$ the closure of $\circ$.

Part 2: Suppose that $\circ$ satisfies *consistency*. Let α be consistent. Then $B\circ\alpha$ is consistent, and hence so is its logical closure $\mathbf{K}*\alpha$.

Part 4: Suppose that $\circ$ satisfies *inconsistent expansion*. Let $\neg\alpha \in \mathrm{Cn}(\varnothing)$. We then have:

$B\circ\alpha = B\cup\{\alpha\}$.

$\mathrm{Cn}(B\circ\alpha) = \mathrm{Cn}(B\cup\{\alpha\})$

$\mathrm{Cn}(B\circ\alpha) = \mathrm{Cn}(\mathrm{Cn}(B)\cup\{\alpha\})$ (properties of Cn)

$\mathbf{K}*\alpha = \mathrm{Cn}(\mathbf{K}\cup\{\alpha\})$

$\mathbf{K}*\alpha = \mathbf{K}+\alpha$

Part 5: Suppose that $\circ$ satisfies *vacuity*: Let $\neg\alpha \notin \mathrm{Cn}(\mathbf{K})$. Since $\mathrm{Cn}(\mathbf{K}) = \mathrm{Cn}(B)$, we then have then $B\circ\alpha = B\cup\{\alpha\}$, and it follows in the same way as in Part 4 that $\mathbf{K}*\alpha = \mathbf{K}+\alpha$.

Part 7: Suppose that $\neg\beta \notin \mathrm{Cn}(\mathbf{K}*\alpha)$. It follows that $\neg\beta \notin \mathrm{Cn}(B\circ\alpha)$. Since $\circ$ satisfies *subexpansion*, we then have:

$(B\circ\alpha)\cup\{\beta\} \subseteq B\circ(\alpha\&\beta)$

$\mathrm{Cn}((B\circ\alpha)\cup\{\beta\}) \subseteq \mathrm{Cn}(B\circ(\alpha\&\beta))$

$\mathrm{Cn}(\mathrm{Cn}(B\circ\alpha)\cup\{\beta\}) \subseteq \mathrm{Cn}(B\circ(\alpha\&\beta))$

$\mathrm{Cn}((\mathbf{K}*\alpha)\cup\{\beta\}) \subseteq \mathbf{K}*(\alpha\&\beta))$

$(\mathbf{K}*\alpha)+\beta \subseteq \mathbf{K}*(\alpha\&\beta))$

206. Let B be a belief base and $\mathbf{K} = \mathrm{Cn}(B)$. Furthermore, let $\circ$ be an operator on B and $*$ the closure of $\circ$. Suppose that $\circ$ satisfies *weak disjunctive inclusion*. We then have for all sentences α and β:

$B\circ(\alpha\vee\beta) \subseteq \mathrm{Cn}((B\circ\alpha)\cup(B\circ\beta))$

$\mathrm{Cn}(B\circ(\alpha\vee\beta)) \subseteq \mathrm{Cn}((B\circ\alpha)\cup(B\circ\beta))$

$\mathrm{Cn}(B\circ(\alpha\vee\beta)) \subseteq \mathrm{Cn}(\mathrm{Cn}(B\circ\alpha)\cup\mathrm{Cn}(B\circ\beta))$

$\mathbf{K}*(\alpha\vee\beta) \subseteq \mathrm{Cn}((\mathbf{K}*\alpha)\cup(\mathbf{K}*\beta))$

207. Let $-$ and $\circ$ be operations on a set B such that $B\circ\alpha = (B-\neg\alpha)\cup\{\alpha\}$ for all α. Furthermore, let $\mathbf{K} = \mathrm{Cn}(B)$, and let $+$ be the closure of $-$ and $*$ the closure of $\circ$. Then:

$\mathbf{K}*\alpha = \mathrm{Cn}(B\circ\alpha)$

$= \mathrm{Cn}((B{-}{-}\neg\alpha)\cup\{\alpha\})$
$= \mathrm{Cn}(\mathrm{Cn}(B{-}{-}\neg\alpha)\cup\{\alpha\})$
$= \mathrm{Cn}((\mathbf{K}\div\neg\alpha)\cup\{\alpha\})$
$= (\mathbf{K}\div\neg\alpha)+\alpha$

208. Let $*$ be the operation such that for all β:
$\mathbf{K}*\beta = (\mathbf{K}\div\neg\beta)+\beta$.
Then, since $\div$ is the closure of $\sim_\gamma$, $\mathbf{K}*\beta = \mathrm{Cn}((B\sim_\gamma\neg\beta)\cup\{\beta\}) = \mathrm{Cn}(B\mp_\gamma\beta)$. It follows from Observation 4.18 that $*$ is an operator of partial meet revision on **K**, and from Observation 3.15 that $\mathbf{K}\cap(\mathbf{K}*\neg\alpha)$ is an operator of partial meet contraction on **K**. Since $\mathbf{K}\cap(\mathbf{K}*\neg\alpha) = \mathbf{K}\cap((\mathbf{K}\div\alpha)+\neg\alpha) = \mathbf{K}\div'\alpha$, this is sufficient to prove that $\div'$ is an operator of partial meet contraction for **K**.

SOLUTIONS FOR CHAPTER 5^{+}

209. According to *incompleteness*, we can let $\alpha \notin$ **K** and $\neg\alpha \notin$ **K**.

It follows from *contraction-vacuity* that **K**$\div\neg\alpha$ = **K**. Applying the *Levi identity* to this, we obtain **K**$*\alpha$ = **K**$+\alpha$. Since $\alpha \in$ **K**$+\alpha$, it follows from *closure under Poss* that $\neg\Diamond\neg\alpha \in$ **K**$+\alpha$.

Applying *closure under Poss* to $\alpha \notin$ **K**, we obtain $\Diamond\neg\alpha \in$ **K**. Since **K** $\subseteq$ **K**$+\alpha$, it follows that $\Diamond\neg\alpha \in$ **K**$+\alpha$.

We have shown that both $\neg\Diamond\neg\alpha$ and $\Diamond\neg\alpha$ are elements of **K**$+\alpha$ and that **K**$*\alpha$ = **K**$+\alpha$; thus **K**$*\alpha$ is inconsistent.

It follows from $\neg\alpha \notin$ **K**, since **K** is logically closed, that $\neg\alpha$ is not logically true. Thus α is consistent. We have already shown that **K**$*\alpha$ is inconsistent. This contradicts *consistency*, and thereby concludes our proof.

210. Yes. In the proof, *consistency* is only applied to prove that (**K**$*\alpha$)$*(\beta\vee\delta)$ is are consistent. It can be replaced by *weak consistency*, as follows:

Since **K** and α are both consistent, it follows from *weak consistency* that **K**$*\alpha$ is consistent. Thus, both **K**$*\alpha$ and $\beta\vee\delta$ are consistent, and it follows from *weak consistency* that (**K**$*\alpha$)$*(\beta\vee\delta)$ is consistent.